STONES

Remembering The Blessings of God

Don Horne

Help Publish Me USA

ISBN-13:978-0692305423
ISBN-10:0692305424

First edition published by
Help Publish Me USA
Waxahachie, Texas
www.helppublish.me

Dedication

My family, especially my wife, and friends have supported me through this and all my endeavors to leave a legacy for the next generation. I dedicate this book to them and to you the reader. I pray the anointing and Grace of Jesus on you promised in Ephesians 4:29 where we can bless one another, and even obtain God's Grace by a positive confession to one another: we are so blessed.

Preface

There are several places in the Old Testament the Lord told the people to set up "Stones" for significant events. These "monuments" were testimonies for what God had done. This book is compiled of "Stones" from a number of different sources. Included are Bible verses, poetry, songs, and powerful testimonies from believers who walk with the Lord.

From the Book of Joshua we read, "After the death of Moses, God made Joshua the leader of the Children of Israel. He was told by God to cross the River Jordan, lead them into the Promised Land, and conquer the surrounding nations. Thus, he would secure the nation of Israel forever."

The River Jordan was at flood stage as it often is at harvest time, and they camped beside the river. After three days, Joshua and the officers came through the camp and said, "When you see the ark of the covenant of the Lord your God, and the priests, who are Levites, carrying it, you are to move out and follow it. Then you will know which way to go, since you have never been this way before. But keep a distance of about a thousand yards between you and the ark; do not go near it." (Holding the very presence of God, the ark was too powerful to even approach.)

Joshua told the people, "Consecrate yourselves, for tomorrow the Lord will do amazing things for you!"

I can imagine an old fashioned night of revival where they prayed and sang. Joshua did not tell them to worry. Instead, he told them to consecrate themselves; to prepare for battle. These young people already were a lean and mighty force that had overcome hard times. I have no doubt they did not spend the night wringing their hands and asking God what to do. He had already told them His plans, and the anticipation of seeing God move had to be a mighty experience.

Joshua told the priests, "When you reach the edge of the Jordan's waters, go and stand in the river."

Joshua told the Israelites, "Come here and listen to the words of the Lord your

God. This is how you will know that the living God is among you and that he will certainly drive out before you the Canaanites, Hittites, Hivites, Perizzites, Girgashites, Amorites, and Jebusites. See, the Ark of the Covenant of the Lord of all the earth will go into the Jordan ahead of you."

Are there any "ites" in your life? God will lead you and help you overcome them all! This is a promise from God!

As soon as the priests carrying the ark reached the Jordan and their feet touched the water's edge, the water from upstream stopped flowing. It piled up in a heap a great distance away, at a town called Adam, in the vicinity of Zarethan, while the water flowing down to the Sea of the Arabah (the Dead Sea) was completely cut off. The priests who carried the Ark of the Covenant stood firm on dry ground in the middle of the Jordan!

When the whole nation had finished crossing the Jordan, the Lord said to Joshua, "Choose twelve people from among the people, one from each tribe, and tell them to pick up twelve stones from the middle of the Jordan where the priests stood and to carry them over with you and put them down at the place where you stay tonight."

So Joshua called together the twelve men he had appointed from the Israelites, one from each tribe, and said to them, "Go over before the ark of the Lord your God into the middle of the Jordan. Each of you is to take a stone on his shoulder, according to the number of the tribes of the Israelites, to serve as a sign among you."

So the Israelites did as Joshua commanded them. They took twelve stones from the middle of the Jordan, according to the number of the tribes of the Israelites, as the Lord had told Joshua. They carried the stones with them over the river to their camp a short distance away, where they put them down.

Then the Lord said to Joshua, "Command the priests carrying the ark to come up out of the Jordan."

So Joshua commanded the priests, "Come up out of the Jordan."

No sooner had they set their feet on the dry ground than the waters of the Jordan returned to their place and ran at flood stage as before.

The people went up from the Jordan and camped at Gilgal where Joshua set up the twelve stones they had taken out of the Jordan.

He said to the Israelites, "In the future, when your children ask you, *'What do these stones mean?'* Tell them that the flow of the Jordan was cut off before the Ark of the Lord. When it crossed the Jordan, the waters of the Jordan were cut off. The Lord your God did to the Jordan just what he had done to the Red Sea when he dried it up for us until we had crossed over. *He did this so that all the peoples of the earth might know that the hand of the Lord is powerful and so that you might always fear the Lord your God.*"

How awesome, when we believe and trust God in the midst of whatever it is we are facing. He moves as we wade right in and see God pile up our troubles from the first to the last and we are allowed to stand on firm, dry ground!

I read this story in the Bible, and I thought about how God is using a new generation of people willing to consecrate themselves and follow Him. He buried the whiners and unbelievers in the desert. He led them out of Egypt, but for unbelief and sin denied the Promised Land to them. Even Moses was denied for disobeying God.

The Israelites entering the river and going into the Promised Land were a hardened, trained, determined force with God Himself in the lead. They would conquer the entire known world as long as they obeyed and trusted God!

Hopefully, this book will be a source of strength and blessing to all who read it. I am leaving it as a legacy to you, especially to my children and grandchildren, to see what God has done in my life and in the lives of others in times past. If He would do it then, He can, and will, do it now.

Stones

My dad was a deacon in Little Rock, Arkansas, at Gaines Street Baptist church when I was young, and he led me through the Sinner's Prayer one Sunday morning when I was 11 years old. (The Sinner's Prayer is the name given to the prayer when we ask God to save us and we believe on His son, Jesus.) Gaines Street Baptist Church lived up to its name, and I was baptized into the Kingdom of God the very next Sunday morning!

I started to carry my Bible to Sunday school, and I was diligent about memorizing the memory verse to make a 100 per cent on the offering envelope. We sang the Books of the Bible every Sunday, and to this day I credit the song for teaching me the location of all the books.

Conversion changed me from a nice young man to a nice young *Christian* man. Even old people were polite to me. I was asked to come help cut lawns, rake leaves, and carry away debris. I did not say no very often, and the pay was not very great. However, to have a <u>little</u> pay in those days was appreciated. I always had enough for a nickel coke and candy bar for my friends and me. That made me popular. I started to see early on some of the benefits of being a Christian young person!

I read my Bible on a daily basis. I confess it was not to just study the Word as much as I enjoyed the Bible Stories. I was a big fan of heroes such as David, Samson, Moses, Joshua, and Daniel. We did not have a TV and I read books all the time. I won a reading award for the most books read every summer at the Little Rock Boys Club.

As a teenager I had a lot of friends and played baseball and football through high school. I was just a normal young man. The threat of my dad's belt stopped me from doing things my peers tried to get me to do.

Once, just a few days after my baptism, my sister and I had an argument that somehow my mother construed as my fault. She told me she was going to go get my dad's belt and whip me. As she left the room, I ran into the bathroom and started praying an "effectual, fervent prayer!" My sister began to dance around and taunt me with, "You are going to get a whipping, ha, ha, ha!"

My mother heard my sister from the doorway and saw me with my eyes tightly shut and my hands folded praying earnestly. Not only did God answer my first prayer by not letting her whip me, but my sister got the spanking! She still has never forgiven me.

In the days of "stand and deliver" I found I had an above average ability to remember and memorize the written Word. The Christmas of my 13th year I memorized and quoted in front of the church the Christmas Story from the 2nd chapter of Luke. My grandmother lived in Centerville, in Northwest Arkansas, where we spent every Christmas holiday. I was asked to recite during the Christmas church service for her church also.

In my quest to set up "Stones" from my life for my family and friends to follow, I want them to settle it in their hearts: God is real and He is a "Rewarder of them which diligently seek Him."

I went to the Navy after a year of college. I had not found a major I really wanted to pursue and whatever I was searching for was not there. It was "out there." I turned 21 aboard the carrier USS Kitty Hawk in Viet Nam. My mother was happily surprised the only thing I wanted was a Bible for my birthday. She signed the fly leaf about how proud she was of me.

I returned from Viet Nam and went back to college at Tennessee Tech in Cookeville, Tennessee. I was the leader of the Young People's Group at the First Assembly of God.

We studied a unit about the Baptism of the Holy Spirit with the initial evidence of "speaking in tongues." During an altar service at the end of a Sunday evening message, I asked God, "If there is something more I can receive from You, I am asking for it now."

I raised my hands with tears flowing to praise Him, and I began speaking in another language! Being yielded to Him was the key. From that day forward I have had a hunger for more of the Word and His Spirit than ever before. I have a library of books from other people who did the same, and I have read the Bible through several times. Like my mother's chocolate pie, I have never gotten my fill! The Holy Spirit Baptism is an important Stone.

Just out of college I was selling cars in Little Rock, Arkansas, and I went for an interview with a Jewish man named Shelly Rand who wanted a manager trainee. Before the interview started I saw him start to empty the trash. I took the basket out of his hand and told him to go ahead and interview the others and I would do it for him. I did not think anything about it. I was just helping him out. When I did not hear from him after a few days, I got down on my knees to ask the Lord to give me that job. The phone started ringing while I was still on my knees. It was Shelly offering the position! Knowing to pray and being willing to help others is another important Stone.

Shelly went out of business, but a friend of his wanted to open a tuxedo rental business in Little Rock. I went to work for

Lou Hoffman's and we soon had a thriving business.

A clothing vendor for Hoffman's who serviced large department stores told a man at Foley's Department Store in Houston about me and I was invited to come to an interview. I was unsure because there were so many candidates, but I went. Out of 150 or so I was invited back. The second time they bought me an airline ticket from Little Rock to Houston. At the second interview I was asked, "Why should we offer this job to you? We have a lot of good people right here at Foley's already. What makes you special?" I knew but I just smiled.

"You are trying to start a formal wear business from scratch, and you need someone that has done it successfully. I have."

I flew home from Houston that day with the job offer in my hand! Being unafraid to trust God and let it be known you are a Christian is a very important Stone.

The next few years I worked for Foley's until they decided renting formal wear was cutting into their sales of formal wear. I prayed for direction, and God immediately gave me a manager trainee's position with Cook Paint of Houston. I trained for a year and they gave me one of the worst stores they had. A year later my store was number one in sales and profit in the company. Trust where God sends you is the next Stone.

I met my wife while working at Cook Paint. We went to church together, and not only was she beautiful physically, she was beautiful on the inside. There could never be a person with a more pure heart than Dilly (DaLoma). She is the wife the wise Solomon described in Proverbs 31:29-30: *"Many women do noble things, but you surpass them all! Charm is deceptive and beauty fleeting, but a woman who fears the Lord is to be praised."* To find a Spirit filled companion to share your life is an important Stone. It is better to walk away now than have to run away later.

God has been very good to us. We have three Godly children and five beautiful granddaughters. God has healed, provided direction and wisdom through the years. Most of all, He has never failed. The next Stone is to trust God completely.

I have more people who ask about, or who want to share with me, testimonies for God's healing than any other topic. I want to give you God's Word about healing first; followed by "Stones" or testimonies from people who God healed.

God's Will to Heal

How do we know whether it's God's will to heal us or not? It makes little difference what others say about it. What did He say about it? These statements are taken directly from the Bible with little or no variation. The verbs and construction have been changed to apply to you personally.

101 Things God Said
Old Testament

God said…

1) I am the Lord that healeth thee. (Ex. 15:26)

2) Your days shall be one hundred and twenty years. (Gen. 6:3)

3) You shall be buried in a good old age (Gen. 15:15)

4) You shall come to your grave in a full age like as a shock of corn cometh in his season. (Job 5:260

5) When I see the blood, I will pass over you and the plague shall not be upon you to destroy you. (Ex. 12:13)

6) I will take sickness away from the

midst of you and the number of your days I will fulfill. (Ex 23:25-26)

7) I will not put any of the diseases you are afraid of on you, but I will take all sickness away from you. (Deut. 7:15)

8) It will be well with you and your days shall be multiplied and prolonged as the days of heaven upon the earth. (Deut. 11: 9,21)

9) I turned the curse into a blessing unto you, because I loved you. (Deut. 23:5 and Neh. 13:2)

10) I have redeemed you from every sickness and every plague. (Deut. 28:61 and Gal. 3:13)

11) As your days, so shall your strength

be. (Deut. 33:25)

12) I have healed you and brought up your soul from the grave; I have kept you alive from going down into the pit. (Ps. 30:1,2)

13) I have found a ransom for you, your flesh shall be fresher than a child's and you shall return to the days of your youth. (Job 33:24,25)

14) I will preserve you and keep you alive. (Ps. 41:2)

15) I will give you strength and bless you with peace. (Ps. 29:11)

16) I will strengthen you upon a bed of languishing; I will turn all your bed in your sickness. (Ps. 41:3)

17) I am the health of your countenance

and your God. (Ps. 43:5)

18) No plague shall come near your dwelling. (Ps. 91:10)

19) I will satisfy you with long life. (Ps. 91:16)

20) I heal all your diseases. (Ps. 103:3)

21) I sent My Word and healed you and delivered you from your destructions. (Ps. 107:20)

22) You shall not die, but live, and declare my works. (Ps. 118:17)

23) I heal your broken heart and bind up your wounds. (Ps. 147:3)

24) The years of your life shall be many. (Pr. 4:10)

25) Trusting Me brings health to your navel and marrow to your bones. (Pr.

3:8)

26) My words are life to you, and health/medicine to all your flesh. (Pr. 4:22)

27) My good report makes all your bones fat. (Pr. 15:30)

28) My pleasant words are sweet to your soul and health to your bones. (Pr. 16:24)

29) My joy is your strength. A merry heart doeth good like a medicine. (Neh. 8:10, Pr. 17:22)

30) The eyes of the blind shall be opened. The eyes of them that see shall not be dim. (Isa. 32:3, 35:5)

31) The ears of the deaf shall be unstopped. The ears of them that

hear shall hearken. (Isa. 32:3, 35:5)

32) The tongue of the dumb shall sing.
The tongue of the stammerers shall
be ready to speak plainly. (Isa. 35:6,
32:4)

33) The lame man shall leap as a hart.
(Isa. 35:6)

34) I will recover you and make you to
live. I am ready to save you. (Isa.
38:16, 20)

35) I give power to the faint. I increase
strength to them that have no might.
(Isa. 40:29)

36) I will renew your strength. I will
strengthen and help you. (Isa. 40:31,
41:10)

37) To your old age and gray hairs I will

carry you and I will deliver you. (Isa. 46:4)

38) I bore your sickness. (Isa. 53:4)

39) I carried your pains. (Isa. 53:4)

40) I was put to sickness for you. (Isa. 53:10)

41) With my stripes you are healed. (Isa. 53:5)

42) I will heal you. (Isa. 57:19)

43) Your light shall break forth as the morning and your health shall spring forth speedily. (Isa. 58:8)

44) I will restore health unto you, and I will heal you of your wounds saith the Lord. (Jer. 30:17)

45) Behold I will heal and mend them. I will make them whole with an

abundance of peace and security. (Jer. 33:6)

46) I will bind up that which was broken and will strengthen that which was sick. (Eze. 34:16)

47) Behold, I will cause breath to enter into you and you shall live. And I will put my Spirit in you and you shall live. (Eze. 37:5)

48) Wherever the river flows, every living thing that moves will thrive. (Eze. 47:9)

49) Seek me and you shall live. (Amos 5:4,8)

50) I have arisen with healing in my wings (beams). (Mal. 4:2)

New Testament

51) I will, be thou clean. (Mt. 8:3)

52) I took your infirmities. (Mt. 8:17)

53) I bore your sicknesses. (Mt. 8:17)

54) If you are sick you need a physician. (I am the Lord your physician.) (Mt. 9:12, Ex. 15:26)

55) I am moved with compassion toward the sick and I heal them. (Mt. 14:14)

56) I heal all manner of sickness and all manner of disease. (Mt. 4:23)

57) According to your faith be it unto you. (Mt. 9:29)

58) I give you power and authority over all unclean spirits to cast them out, and to heal all manner of sickness and all manner of disease. (Mt. 10:1,

Lk.9:1)

59) I heal them all. (Mt. 12:15, Heb. 13:8)

60) As many as touch Me are made perfectly whole. (Mt. 14:36)

61) Healing is the children's bread. (Mt. 15:26)

62) I do all things well. I make the deaf to hear and the dumb to speak. (Mk 7:37)

63) If you can believe, all things are possible to him that believeth. (Mk. 9:23)

64) When hands are laid on you, you shall recover. (Mk. 16:18)

65) My anointing heals the brokenhearted, and delivers the

captives, recovers sight to the blind, and sets at liberty those that are bruised. (Lk. 4:18, Isa. 10:27, 61:1)

66) I heal all those who have need of healing. (Lk. 9:11)

67) I am come not to destroy men's lives, but to save them. (Lk. 9:56)

68) Behold, I give you authority over all the enemy's power and nothing by any means shall hurt you. (Lk. 10:19)

69) Sickness is satanic bondage and you ought to be loosed today! (Lk. 13:16 & II Cor. 6:2)

70) In Me is life. (Jn. 1:4)

71) I am the bread of life. I give you life. (Jn. 6:33,35)

72) The Words I speak unto you are spirit and life. (Jn. 6:63)

73) I am come that you might have life and that you might have it more abundantly. (Jn. 10:10)

74) I am the resurrection and the life. (Jn. 11:25)

75) If you ask anything in my name I will do it. (Jn. 14:14)

76) Faith in my name makes you strong and gives you perfect soundness. (Acts 3:16)

77) I stretch forth my hand to heal. (Acts 4:30)

78) I, Jesus Christ, make you whole. (Acts 9:34)

79) I do good and heal all that are

oppressed of the devil. (Acts 10:38)

80) My power causes diseases to depart from you. (Acts 19:12)

81) The law of the spirit in Me has made you free from the law of sin and death. (Rom. 8:2)

82) The same spirit that raised Me from the dead now lives in you and will quicken your mortal body. (Rom. 8:11)

83) Your body is a member of Me. (I Cor. 6:15)

84) Your body is the temple of My Spirit and you are to glorify Me in your body. (I Cor. 6:19,20)

85) If you'll rightly discern My body which was broken for you, and judge

yourself, you will not be judged and you will not be weak, sickly, or die prematurely. (I Cor. 11:29-31)

86) I have set gifts of healing in My body. (I Cor. 12:9)

87) My life may be made manifest in your mortal body. (II Cor. 4:10,11)

88) I have delivered you from death, I do deliver you, and if you will trust Me I will yet deliver you. (II Cor. 1:10)

89) I have given you My name and put all things under your feet. (Eph. 1:21, 22)

90) I want it to be well with you and I want you live long on the earth. (Eph. 6:3)

91) I have delivered you from the

authority of darkness. (Col. 1:13)

92) I will deliver you from every evil work. (II Tim. 4:18)

93) I tasted death for you. I destroyed the devil who had the power of death. I've delivered you from the fear of death and bondage. (Heb. 2: 9, 14, 15)

94) I wash your body with pure water. (Heb. 10:22, Eph. 5:26)

95) Lift up the weak hands and the feeble knees. Don't let that which is lame be turned aside but rather let Me heal it. (Heb. 12:12, 13)

96) Let the elders anoint you and pray for you in My name and I will raise you up. (Jas. 5: 14,15)

97) Pray for one another and I will heal you. (Jas. 5: 16)

98) By My stripes you were healed. (I Pet. 2: 24)

99) My Divine power has given unto you all things that pertain to life and godliness through the knowledge of me. (II Pet. 1:3)

100) Whosoever will let him come and take of the water of life freely. (Rev. 22:7)

101) Beloved, I wish above all things that you may...be in health. (III Jn. 2)

Foreword

I realized where I wanted to go with this book, and there are already a number of books about testimonies including several of my own. However, I wanted to end up with a more definitive book which dealt with the absolute miracles from God in which every Christian can relate.

These "Stones" or "monuments" are important enough in our walk with the Lord to overcome satan, according to Revelation 12:11; *"They overcame him by the blood of the lamb and the Word of their testimonies."*

God told Joshua to set these up as if He also thought it was important. God does not want us to forget what He has done in the past. It can increase our Faith to receive from Him today in any area of our life.

The "Stones" for healing are of prime importance to most of us, and I begin with a healing from cancer to a friend of mine. There are testimonies about God healing a deformed baby, and even one brought back to life. God is on the throne to take your requests!

Healed From Cancer

Kay Bonds

This testimony begins in 1985 when I first had a brain aneurysm. Many doctors tried but could not determine what was wrong with me. I did not have the usual symptoms of a brain aneurysm. They finally did a CAT Scan after several months of other tests. This scan showed a real probability of a brain aneurysm. An arteriogram proved the brain aneurysm was there on the left side. Surgery was performed and during surgery they found the aneurysm had already leaked blood. I should have had a stroke, been incapacitated, or died. I recovered fully from the surgery with absolutely no side effects. It was a true miracle I survived with no ill effects.

A Christian gentleman from my office at Xerox said I had a testimony to tell, and this would be a good chance to witness to others about the power of God. I agreed. I had been saved as a child, went to church, church camp, etc. It seems, however, at this time of my life I thought I was too busy to follow up with what God wanted me to do.

When I was diagnosed with Breast Cancer in 2011, I realized this was another opportunity to be a witness that God is with us always. I started reading healing scriptures every day which had been sent when my husband was diagnosed with cancer in 2009. These scriptures sustained me day by day.

After I was diagnosed with Breast Cancer, I had the usual mammograms, sonograms, and various other tests including biopsy before surgery. Surgery followed with a month for recovery before Chemotherapy started. I considered not having any treatment plans. The doctor said the pathology report showed no cancer around where the surgery had been performed. I knew God had already healed me. My husband had passed away in 2009, and I felt I was ready to go to Paradise. God let me know a cancer death is not a pretty death, and certainly not what He had in store for me. Very soon I decided to have both

Chemo and Radiation Therapy as a preventive measure. I was at perfect peace with this decision.

My first four Chemo treatments (two different kinds of Chemo) at Baylor Texas Oncology in Waxahachie on Thursdays followed by a shot on Fridays at Baylor Texas Oncology Dallas were not bad at all. I don't mean I highly recommend it, but I never got sick. The summer of 2011, however, was so hot it made recovery from each treatment every other week harder to get over than it would have if it had been a bit cooler.

The last four treatments involved a new Chemo on Thursdays in Waxahachie followed by the same shot on Fridays in Dallas. The first one was such a shock to my system! It immediately gave me Neuropathy (a disease of the nerve endings) in both my hands/fingers and feet/toes. I could hardly walk or use my hands because of the pain. I thought I must stop treatment at that point, and talked to the Oncologist about it over the weekend.

The next day, which was a Sunday, "I sought the Lord and He heard me, and delivered me from all my fears." (Psalm 34:4). I knew I must go on. After all God said He would give me strength and peace my entire life. In 2011 I actually felt that strength and peace surround me. I repented that weekend that I let go of the strength and peace which God had provided me. I read Psalm 29:11 again which says, "I will give you strength and bless you with peace." I received His blessings and praise Him for it every day.

I went on to finish my Chemo with God's help. I was given a month off before starting Radiation to rebuild my body. My Chemo Oncologist was very pleased with my progress, and even said I was a very pleasant patient to have around. Of course, I did bring cookies to the Doctor and nurses every day I had treatment! I still take cookies on my follow-up visits.

I started my Radiation after much preparation. I went to Charlton Methodist Texas Oncology in Duncanville every day for 35 days. I was pretty burned up on the outside, but I knew God had new skin in store for me. I finished my Radiation treatments a week before Christmas. I was able to make Christmas dinner for my sister (a widow also) and me. Maybe not the best we've had over the years, but quite good even if I do say so myself. By the way, I don't think I mentioned I work 5 to 6 hours a day, or as needed in Red Oak. I continued to work the entire time I was receiving treatments. I did have a day or two I went home early, but God kept me working. I consider that to be a testimony in itself!

I am doing great now. I am just waiting on hair, eyebrows, and eyelashes to grow back. I was taking a pill once a day the

Oncologist wanted me to take for 5 years. I believe it was causing what hair, eyebrows, and eyelashes that had been growing stop growing. He took me off the medication for a couple of months to see how it went. I told him I was already healed.

I could have started this testimony back in 1981 when my husband went to rehab for alcohol and prescription drug addiction. That is when we really started back on the path God had for us. Both of us grew up in Christian homes, but had strayed from God for a while. When my husband, Andy, came home from rehab, we both knew God was taking care of us, but we did not take the opportunity to witness another miracle. Andy said one day he felt God lift the desire for alcohol from his body and spirit. He stayed sober the rest of his life. When cancer struck me, even before tests, surgery, and treatment; I knew I must give witness to the goodness of God and how He helps me live every day on this earth. God loves us and wants us to not only be healed when we are sick, but He wants us well and living in Divine health and living strong every day of our lives.

The next few Stones I would best describe as "Give your all to God, and let Him direct your life." They are great testimonies from my friend, Herb Corpany. At the young age of 85 he still loves to sing in church and win people to Jesus. Read this group of sermons as a blueprint on how to serve God.

~Editor

My Journey Through The Eye Of The Needle

I accepted the Lord as my Savior in April of 1944 at the age of 17 in Pecos,

Texas. My hometown was Brenham, Texas. I moved to Pecos 550 miles away when the company I worked for transferred me.

There has been an interest all my life in going to church, but I had really never made a commitment. The first Saturday in Pecos I went by myself to a movie named, "Stormy Weather." The other men on my work team went to the bars. Upon leaving the theater, a man gave me a small booklet of John's Gospel from the Bible. I read all of it two or three times that night. The Holy Spirit used this as well as the storms of destruction in the movie to drive me to my knees. I asked for forgiveness for my sins and asked God to lead me by His Spirit. I learned more later about the process in Mark 10:25.

I got up early the next morning and drove around town looking for a church, passing by several. I felt led to stop at one where the sign read "Assembly of God." At 7:30 AM in the morning I knocked on the door of the house next door. I asked the lady, "What time do they have Sunday School and Church?" She told me and I said, "I think I will come." I did.

They had songs and a few testimonies followed by a message from a young, visiting preacher stationed at the Pecos Air Force Base. He gave an altar call and I responded. As soon as my knees touched the floor, I cried out for Jesus to forgive me of my sins and come into my heart, just as I had done the night before. This time I felt total peace, including joy, happiness and a relationship with God and His Church. I hugged everyone in sight because I was happy, and I still am.

I spiritually went through the gate spoken of in Mark 10:25 concerning *"the eye of the needle."* The desire of my heart was to know God and His peace. Before the camel could go through *"the eye of the needle"* to enter the city, everything had to be removed from it. This was a good place for the tax assessor to assess the value of the merchandise the camel was carrying.

When we turn our lives over to God, we let go of our baggage and leave it outside the gate. The next time our surveying party went to survey the land and set benchmarks, I said to myself and some of my co-workers, "I am so content for this is what I have been looking for."

The next Sunday, I learned about the infilling of the Holy Spirit (Mark 1:8). John said, "I indeed have baptized you with water, but He, the Christ, shall baptize you with the Holy Spirit and with fire." (Matthew 3:11)

I said, "Lord, you gave me what I asked for last Sunday, but my heart is heavy. I desire and long to be baptized with the Holy Spirit and fire." I bowed low before God and went through the gate another time.

I yielded my whole spirit and tongue to God's will for my life.

He said, "Receive and you shall have My baptism and fire." I received. The Glory of God is wonderful!

Sister Gaither, a dear lady in the Pecos Church, took me under her wing and taught me how to sing solos at her church. She told me I had to memorize the songs though. I had praise in my spirit and a song in my heart. She also required and urged me to come to her home for prayer every morning at 6:00 AM.

Again, I bowed low before God and asked for His anointing, for His glory alone. God said, *"Go, my son, and sing my songs, and I will burn My word into the hearts of men."* I was requested to sing at my home church, area youth rallies, fellowship meetings, and the Big Springs Camp Meeting. I felt good being used of God. While men were praising God and glorifying His name, I had nothing but praise for His presence. I did not realize I had more gates of humility to go through.

A few weeks later, I attended a C.A. Rally in Monahans, Texas, where I received a strong desire to speak to men the Word of God they might receive what I had. God said, *"Go through my gate, and I will be with you."* The group I was working with moved to North Dakota, but a family connected with the church offered me a job delivering ice cream to other towns in West Texas.

While driving a large truck full of ice cream and nickel novelties, on Highway 17 to Fort Davis and Marfa, I passed a large ranch house with about 10 smaller houses around it. I went up to the houses and asked the children to come out and receive a stick of ice cream.

I gave each one a stick of ice cream and then I asked, "Would you like to hear a Bible story?" I spoke the Word and their hearts were made whole. They loved God, me, and the ice cream. I made the trip once a week. God used the blessing of ice cream to bring several young people to Christ.

Early in 1945, I was drafted into the U.S. Army and sent to the South Pacific and then to Japan. As soon as I arrived in Japan I went to my secret chamber and bowed low before God. I asked for Him to show me a way to reach the Japanese people. He said, *"Listen to my Spirit and you will find a way."*

I was a radio operator, and a few nights later, I was on the big radio we had there to see what I could pick up. While I was in Tokyo, I picked up a program coming out of South America called, *Back To The Bible Broadcast.* They announced they would send Gospel tracts in the Japanese language to anyone who would give them out. I said, *"Yes, Lord. That's it!"*

I would stand on the corner one block from the Ginza Street Methodist Church and point to the church and tell them we would be having services Saturday night.

One of my soldier buddies saw me handing out tracts. He came up to me and said, *"You big sissy. You are nothing but a weakling. You are a disgrace to our outfit."*

I said back to him, *"If you are so strong, here, you pass them out."* He hurried off and left me alone.

After being discharged from the Army, I returned home to attend Southwestern, T.C.U., and Midwestern University. While attending Southwestern again, I bowed low and asked God for a wife who could, and would, help me with my ministry of preaching, singing, and teaching other Christians to win souls. He said, *"My son, I have given you the things you have desired for my Glory. Go and I will send you a wife who will be a helpmate to glorify me."* He did. Soon after arriving at Southwestern, I met Ruby. We married a year and a half later on the night she graduated from High School. Two weeks later we began pastoring a church: I was 21 and Ruby was 17. God gave us two wonderful children who love and serve God as well as grandchildren who are involved in ministry.

In January 1994, there was a revival at Oak Cliff Assembly of God in Dallas, Texas, led by Evangelist Mike Evans. The

Lord used me in many ways to glorify His name, but my heart became broken and unsatisfied. One more time a gracious and loving God visited me in a mighty way. He asked, *"What is it you desire?"* I bowed low before Him with a brokenness of heart, and said, *"Only the things that You desire to give unto me."* I was on my back in the altar area and could not get up because the glory was so strong and my body was so weak. God said, *"Come with me and I will take you on a journey."* We passed through, in the Spirit, the anointed preaching, the anointed singing, my pastoral experience, and into a place where only God and I were.

I said, *"God, I am willing to do what you want me to do."* He took me to a place where men and women must come if their heart's cry is to be fulfilled. Looking back, I see that again I bowed low before a gate called *"The Eye Of The Needle"* (Mark 10:25)

The Spirit of God said, *"Bow low."* I bowed low. Then He said, *"Bow lower."* I bowed lower. He said, *"Lower, you are not low enough."* I went as low as I could: all the way flat on my back. On my back I had the Books Of Learning, and I had my gifts and abilities. So, I dropped them to enable me to go through a very small gate called, *"The Eye Of The Needle."* As I arose on the other side, a wonderful thing happened! I felt His presence! I saw His Glory!

I cried, *"God what is this thing you have done to me?"*

He said, *"You have come through the Gate of Worship – Intercessory Prayer."*

While I was still on the floor, God called to my attention the many who were there that had not laid down their talent. They said, *"God gave them to me."* Therefore they would not lay them down. One had his money. Another had his musical instruments. Another his abilities to speak the Word, the ability to organize and accomplish God's program; his past victories with God; his beautiful voice to sing the Gospel; his time of study and prayer that equipped him to write books so others could learn to win souls. They refused to lay everything down. They continued to claim the Glory that belonged to only God. They were allowing the pride of Satan to blind them.

After going through the gate something great was revealed! I looked at the inside part of that small gate of worship and intercessory prayer that I had to give everything up to go through. God's instruments of music were there. His books were there. His Bible sword was there. God's power was there. Now these things are His, not mine.

The Word of God says, and I would add clearly saying, *"If you do not come through the Gate of Worship and Intercessory Prayer, which is very small, I will only be able to minister and bless the hearts of men. But if you will come through the small gate, "the Gate of Worship and Intercessory Prayer," you will rise to the other side, not just to minister to men, but to minister to our great God Jehovah!"*

We were pastors for four churches; one for 27 years. Although age has crept up on me at over 85 years old, I continue to have a strong passion for the sick, discouraged, and those who need to accept Christ. A non-profit organization, "Herb Corpany Ministries," makes it all possible for me to visit approximately 400 people a year.

This continues to be a refreshing message to my life in August 2014.

~Herb Corpany

Nicodemus, The Pharisee

Nicodemus. this name makes one wonder, and remember, the man that came to Jesus by night. But why did he wait until night?

Who was Nicodemus? Some historians connect him to Nicodemus Bar Gorion, the brother of Josephus the Jewish historian. There is no solid evidence for this view so it cannot be stated as a fact.

Nicodemus was a Pharisee. Paul was also a Pharisee and his father was too. (Acts 23:1-6) This was when Paul was before the Sanhedrin, which was the supreme Jewish council and court of justice at Jerusalem in New Testament times. "This council was split down the middle—the Pharisees against the Sadducees." (Acts 23:7)

Who were the Pharisees? They were a group of separatists (Pharisee means "to separate") who rose to prominence during the inter-testament period (the 400 years between the Old and New Testaments.) During this time, Greek influence was very strong throughout the world and many of the Jews who had returned from the Babylonian captivity were living much like their Gentile neighbors. These ultra Orthodox Jews, later called Pharisees, took it upon themselves to find ways to enforce strict observance of Jewish ritual laws. They became the self-imposed conscience of the Jewish people. (Dake's Reference Bible.)

The Church leaders today often condemn the Pharisees, but for the most part, for the wrong reason. We tend to think of them as teaching doctrine error, but their doctrine was rather accurate. They believed in the resurrection of the dead, life after death, angels, and obedience to the laws of God. They placed a priority on the holiness and sovereignty of God and, above all, they separated themselves from any form of idolatry.

Their great mistake was they viewed a proper relationship with God in terms of how carefully a person kept all the rules outwardly. They eternalized religion outwardly, making it a matter of behavior rather than a matter of the heart. This is true of some religious groups today, this zeal and commitment were praiseworthy but their motives were completely wrong.

The Pharisees were serious students of the scriptures, (our Old Testament). They knew what their Bible said. This was revealed in the reply of the chief priests and scribes to Herod's request to find out the Messiah's birthplace. They knew immediately that it was Bethlehem. Many of those priests and scribes no doubt were Pharisees.

All of this tells us a lot about Nicodemus. He was an older gentleman of learning and knowledge. He was considered one of the chief teachers of Israel. He was intensely familiar with the Bible and would have been knowledgeable of these portions that were messianic in nature. He was respected and honored by his peers. This was the man who came to Jesus by night.

Many reasons have been considered for this nighttime visit. The main one is that Nicodemus feared the censure of his peers if they knew that he had approached this despised young Rabbi with questions. This may well have been the case, for peer pressure is a powerful force, even for a man as respected as Nicodemus.

It was suggested that he came by night because that would afford a better opportunity to actually talk with Jesus. During the day Jesus was often surrounded by the multitudes, many looking for physical healing. Nighttime would afford some quality time for the famous Rabbi to converse with the young Rabbi.

Nicodemus had seen and heard of the works of Jesus. His opening words (John 3:2) revealed that he recognized something very special about this man. He could have been under conviction and could not wait until morning. When the Holy Spirit begins to work on a person's heart, that too, results in some kind of action. This is what happened to me in Pecos, Texas, one Saturday night in 1943.

This may be the reason that Jesus, during his discourses on the thoughts and intents of the heart got to the core of the matter very quickly in verse 3. Jesus knew

Nicodemus' statement –"Rabbi, we know that you are a teacher come from God—for no man can do these miracles that you do except God be with him." (John 3:2) was leading to the question, "What must I do to see or enter the kingdom of God?"

In this we see another side of Nicodemus' character: humility. It must have been a humbling experience for this respected teacher to come to Jesus and say, "We know that thou…" only to have this uneducated, unlettered, untrained, Galilean Rabbi say to him, "No, you don't know. You can see me perform the miracles, but you cannot see or know the kingdom of God until you start over with another birth."

How thankful we should be that Nicodemus swallowed his pride and came by night to the Rock of Ages to get the truth of the ages. It was through this meeting with Jesus that Nicodemus would learn and the world would learn. "God so loved the world that He gave His only begotten son, that whosoever believeth in Him should not perish, but have ever lasting life." (John 3:16)

Christian tradition teaches that Nicodemus became a follower of Jesus and was baptized by Peter and John. Because of his faith in Christ, he lost his Jerusalem home, his wealth, and his position with the Jewish Council (the Sanhedrin).

Nicodemus' 3 steps:

    1.Came to Jesus by night. John 3:2

    2.Testified for him. John 7:50-51

    3.Did service for him. John 19:20

These are examples for us to follow even in this day.

I believe Nicodemus could say like Paul, (2 Tim 4:7)

"I have fought the good fight, I have finished my course, I have kept the faith. (v8) Henceforth there is laid up for me a crown of righteousness, which the Lord, the righteous judge, shall give me at that day,

and not to me only, but unto all of them also that love his appearing."

One   of   God's children,

Herb Corpany

The Prodigal

In Luke 15, Jesus is trying to cause the Pharisees and scribes to break out of their religious shell, so they can get away from the judgmental hard attitude toward publicans, sinners, and anyone else who may disagree with them. The Pharisees had no mercy, and grumbled about miracles performed on the Sabbath. They complained about Jesus eating with sinners, as well as His forgiving them when they brought fruit of forgiveness.

Because of Jesus' great love for the Pharisees, He turns to them and rebukes them three times. In the day Jesus lived, if you rebuke a man once, it's a rebuke. If you rebuke him twice, that's an insult, and if you rebuke him three times, it is absolutely humiliating and crushing. There are many rebukes inside of this one.

It is amazing that Jesus had gone this far dealing with the Pharisees and scribes. Let's look at the scriptures and rehearse the story again. We will just pull out the bare facts.

A father had two sons. The younger came and said, "Give me my share of the inheritance," and the father gave it to him.

Soon the son went into a far country or land, and there he wasted all his substance on wild parties and prostitutes. When his money was gone, there arose a great famine in the land, and he began to starve. He persuaded a farmer to let him take care of his pigs. While feeding the pigs, he became hungry and hurting. He came to himself, and said, "I will arise and go back home where even the hired hands have enough to eat and a little to spare, for I am dying of hunger and it makes no sense at all for me to stay here." He arose and started back home.

His father saw him a long way off and ran to greet him. He gave him the family ring; the robe, shoes, and killed the fatted calf. They began to hold a party, and the older son was very offended at this. The father came out and entreated him, telling him everything he had was his and didn't he want to come in and rejoice with them.

NOW LET'S LOOK AT SOME DETAILS:

There are really three prodigals – the prodigal younger brother, the prodigal father, and the prodigal older brother.

Luke 15:11-12 *"A certain man had two sons. The younger son said to his father, Father, give me the portion of the estate that falleth to me".* He divided unto them his living. (The father agreed to divide his wealth unto his two sons.)

This was a no, no in biblical times, or even the small old villages of the Middle East today. No younger son would ever ask his father for his share of the family's wealth. What this really means is, drop dead, because you do not get your inheritance until the father dies. The younger son is saying to his father, "I wish you were dead, so I could receive my part of the family inheritance right now."

The following came from Kenneth Bailey, who lived in an Arab village for two years to observe and learn the culture of the eastern countries. He also lived in an Israeli village one year, for the same reasons. My brother, B. W. Corpany, knew him personally, as they both lived in Beirut, Lebanon, at the same time. I gave away many of his books, which were, of course, very rich in eastern and Middle Eastern culture.

Kenneth once asked a group of Israeli fathers in a small village what they would do if their young son came and asked for his inheritance. They all replied they would beat him unmercifully because he had greatly insulted them.

There is another matter that must be considered. The father is not only the father of his family, but he is also head of the village. His wealth is also communal wealth, marked by collective ownership and to be used by the entire village.

Now we understand the younger son is asking for his part of wealth that belongs to the whole village. Therefore, when he wasted it, he was affecting the economy of many other people. It should have been kept to benefit the village, such as to build a new house or have a new water system installed that would increase their wealth. Another possibility would have been to place lamps in front of his house that would help light a part of the village. But no, he went to a far country and wasted his inheritance on disorderly behavior. It was a loss to his village.

LOOK AT THIS PRESENT DAY DELIMMA. Many of us are spending our money on things of little or no value. I am referring to eternal value. Think for a moment…"What have you spent on eternal things this week?"

There were three ways the father could give over his estate:

1) When he died.

2) If the father retires totally, he can give everything to the older son. The older son does not actually own the estate, but he is the overseer, the steward. Then the father can relax in the sun, spend time with his grandchildren, or whatever he desires to do. (What a life!)

3) Another way the father can divide his estate is to give a portion of his wealth to his sons and yet retain some authority. That is what this father does in Luke 15:12.

Verse 13: "A few days later this younger son packed all his belongings and took a trip to a distant land."

NOTICE: There are two things here. If there is a problem in the family or a difference of opinion, the elder brother or son is to be the mediator. The elder brother should have stepped into the situation, and been the mediator between the father and the younger son. He should have pleaded with the younger son to be reasonable, and quit wishing their father would die. He should have said, "Don't do this. It is a disgrace to our family."

(PRAISE The LORD... JESUS IS OUR ELDER BROTHER) !!!

I know this wasn't said in the parable, but sometimes what is not said is more important then what is said. The Pharisees knew they were the older brothers and they should be mediators, not judges.

WHAT ABOUT US TODAY? ARE WE MEDIATORS OR JUDGES? WE SHOULD BE PLEADING FOR THE LOST SHEEP OF OUR FAMILY AND COMMUNITIES. ARE WE?

Verse 13) "And not many days later, he gathered all his things together." To do this, he would sell what he couldn't take with him at a cut-rate price. This is another insult to his father and family, because he did not get the true value of the items. It could have been jewelry, clothing, or land. The Pharisees knew, as older brothers, they should be working with and helping the younger. (PLEASE LORD, HELP ME UNDERSTAND THIS.)

In the Middle East in Jesus' day, it was rare for a person to take a trip into a distant country. Most people lived their entire life in and around their own village. Even when one took a trip to a neighboring village, there was a great celebration. They hugged and kissed you upon arrival, and listened with great earnestness at what was going on in your own village. But this young man was different. He was leaving his kind, so he could live as loose as he pleased and that he did.

Verse 13 – *"and there wasted all his money on parties and loose living."* According to Kenneth Bailey, it might not have been as it is today—wine, women, and song. Bailey reminds us that the younger son had no status or importance, which he wanted very much. The younger son is like a servant, but the older son had authority. He could ask the father to have a party and with common consent, they would have one. Not so with the younger son. To feel important, the younger son spent his money on parties, therefore, his money was running out, and there wasn't any more coming in. I can see it now – he is giving to certain people so they will like him. Some may have even given a gift to him in return, which made him feel wanted.   (HOW WE LIKE TO FEEL WANTED OR NEEDED.)

The younger son spent all his money partying and giving gifts. A wise man will save some money for a rainy day. Sure enough, "About the time his money was gone, there arose a great famine in the land, and he began to starve. His condition was so severe that he persuaded a local farmer to hire him to feed his pigs." (verse 15) This revealed his willingness to do anything to keep from starving. His values are changing quickly. He is beginning to see life in its basic form. If he sees the farmer's water pot getting low, he runs to the well and fills it. This is the way he persuaded the farmer to let him work. Just anything, so he can eat and not starve!

Another translation puts verse 15 like this…"He attached himself to one of the citizens of that country and persuaded him to let him feed his pigs." He made a nuisance of himself to the farmer for employment.

Let us go back to verse 14 ... "About the time his money was gone, a great famine swept over the land and he began to starve." A great famine or a mighty famine – either one is terrible and devastating. A famine is when there is a lack of food, water, or anything else that pertains to the basics of life. Sometimes there is plenty of food, but it needs to be released from those who are holding it. (Similar to the lepers outside the Syrian army camp, God intervened.)

Would God ever allow his people to experience a Spiritual famine? Yes, when His people turn from Him, and go after other gods. Do you, like me, feel this is where the U.S.A. is right now? Most spiritual food today is so watered down; it has little or no spiritual strength to it. Much of what is being served has no real energy substance in it. The taste may seem good, but it is hollow calories -- which translates into lack of energy.

The famine and starving condition the young Jewish lad was having made him stop and think. (Verse 17) *"But coming to himself," he said, "how many hired servants of my father have a super abundance of bread and I am perishing with hunger."*

Coming to himself, or coming to his senses, or awakening from his madness and folly, God gives everyone a wake up call, but some can't hear it because the volume of worldly things is turned up so loud.

Let's go back to another point I'd like to bring up. Why did the younger son want to leave home anyway? By what the older brother did, and did not do reveals how he felt about the younger son. He did not try to reason with him and show him what a bad mistake he was making by wishing his father was dead. Jesus brought this point out for the Pharisees, but what about our Pharisaical spirit of today? Plenty of children of professing Christians have been hardened toward the church because of the lack of spiritual leadership and Christian example.'

Also, why did the father divide the inheritance with the young son? Because he understood how the younger son felt about his big brother and home. He could have wondered why his dad didn't call his older brother in, and give him a good talking to. Yes, the father knew the younger son needed to try it on his own. He hoped he would come to his senses. It was because of love the father let him go.

Now we see all three: the father, the older son, and the younger son are all being prodigals. Oh Brother Herb, you are probably thinking, how can you say that? Because it is a fact. The father represents the priesthood of that day. The older son represents the Pharisees, and the younger son represents the gentiles and heathen. Let us be quick to say the true priesthood, THE BELIEVERS IN CHRIST, is revealed in the father when he looks and longs for his prodigal younger son to come to himself, and his household. Can you see the father has disgraced himself by allowing his two sons to be disobedient? (THIS IS WHERE THE CHURCH AT LARGE IS TODAY.)

Not only did the younger son come to himself, but the father also came to himself, and longed for his son's return. How we should all long for our children to come to God with everything that's within them. As the father loved his son in Luke 15:32, we are also to love ours.

As the younger son came to his senses, he rehearsed what he would say when he returned home. Because of the father's outpouring of love on him, he never said all he had planned to. If we could only conceive of how much God the Father loves us, we would never go astray or disobey him in any way. His is a pure love, not up and down like we humans. As humans, we cannot be constant. It is not in our physical or mental ability to be constant.

His plan in verse 18…*I will go to my father, and will say unto him, "Father, I sinned against Heaven and before you. I am no more worthy to be called your son. Make me as one of your hired servants."*

(Verse 20) *"And arising, he came to his father. But while he was yet afar off, his father saw him."*

(LET'S LOOK AT SOME OF THE CULTURE OF THAT DAY.) The father's house was usually built in the center of the village, which meant he could not see someone coming unless he was looking for them. We might also consider the house had almost a flat roof, which was used to relax in the cool of the day. I think the father had sat up there many times since the son had been gone, to look for him.

This reminds me of a time when my family had taken a trip to Egypt in 1973. We spent a few days there, and were ticketed on the airlines to proceed to Beirut, where my brother and family were missionaries. When we presented our tickets at the airport to receive boarding passes, we were told there were no reservations for four Corpanys on neither that flight nor any other. I took a taxi to downtown Cairo (20 miles) to see if our names were in the big computer. They were, but they would not honor them. Later in the day, we found a flight that had two spaces going to Beirut. I took my children out on the tarmac as far as I could for them to board their plane, when a big Egyptian soldier told me to stop and not go any farther. I did not understand his language, but soon I realized he meant for me to stop. In the last moments I had with them, I asked them if they had their passports and boarding passes, or anything else they might need. They said, "Yes, everything is in order." I asked if they had Uncle B. W.'s phone number, and they both said, "Yes, Daddy, we have everything." The soldier looked at me, hit the butt of his rifle against the ground and pointed toward the airport building. I knew he was telling me to go back to the building. After I walked a short distance, I turned around and watched the plane load. The doors were shut, and it soared out of sight. I wondered if I would ever see them again, and if they would be able to contact B.W in Beirut. (The reason we sent them on, and Ruby and I remained in Cairo was because they told us it was impossible for the 4 of us to go on one flight at any time.)

When they arrived in Beirut, they discovered we had all forgotten to send their health cards with them. They were asked to show them, and when they couldn't find them, the airport attendant motioned for them to go on. My daughter saw the slight movement of his hand and told her brother to come on because he was going to let them enter without them.

It was the following day before Ruby and I could get a flight to Beirut. We had not notified them of our arrival, but much to our surprise when we stepped off the plane, they were waving from the balcony shouting: "Corpany! Corpany! Corpany!" It was

Sherrie, Herb and B.W.'s family. I later asked them how did they know we were going to be on that flight? They said that they had met every flight arriving from Cairo.

I can see it now. The father meets every flight. This is also the way the father in Luke 15:20 did. He checked out every person entering the village, anticipating one would be his son.

Jesus said, *"He had come to seek and to save that which was lost. I would that none would perish, and that all would come unto repentance."* (GOD IS SAYING, PLEASE COME HOME.) Luke 15:*20 "And while he was yet a far off, his father saw him, and was moved with compassion;*

and running, he fell on his neck and kissed him much."

In the culture of that people, a person was to arrive in the evening, a little before night. Therefore every evening the father looked intently for the return of his son.

This reminds me of what I was told recently at a graveside service of a man named Mr. Hopkins. They said the previous week he had called the relatives together telling them his departure was at hand. He told them he wished he could work on all their cars to get them in tiptop shape, but his time was almost up, and it was the evening of his life. There is something about wanting to get home before dark.

When we were children in the 30's, living in the country, my mother always had an oil lamp burning in the front window if any member of the family was not at home.

"And running, he fell on his neck and embraced him and kissed him much."

Not only did the father see him, but the other men and older boys saw him, and were ready to throw rocks at him because of the way he had disgraced their village. This again was the culture of that day. He was to be punished for the crime he had committed against his village.

Also, in that culture, no man ran. It was a show of lack of faith. One does not run when he is in control.

The father ran for at least two reasons. He was so glad the boy was coming home, and he wanted to reach him before the men would have an opportunity to stone him. When the father reached the son, he opened his arms wide and took him inside his robe, kissed him, and kept him covered from the stones that had been prepared to use against him.

Isaiah 61:10: "**HE HAS COVERED ME WITH THE ROBE OF RIGHTEOUSNESS**." Can you see this? SATAN HAS PREPARED TO STONE GOD'S CHILDREN TO DEATH, BUT THE COVERING OF HIS ROBE GOD PROVIDES FOR THEM KEEPS HIM FROM IT.

**GOD LOVES YOU SO MUCH!!
WILL YOU ACCEPT IT AND LIVE IN
IT? WILL YOU LET IT SHINE
THROUGH YOU?**

For a few minutes, let us look at the elder son. Verses 25-26) *"Meanwhile, the older son was in the field working. When he returned home, he heard dance music coming from the house and he asked one of the servants what was going on?"* Verse 27: *"Your brother is back, and your father has killed the calf we were fattening and has prepared a great feast to celebrate his coming home unharmed."*

Are you happy when a child has been rescued from death? And what if it were your son? I would be like Jesus said,

"Rejoice when the lost sheep has been found." (Luke 12:4-6) *I would take off a day from my work and be merry, because the sheep was found and is unharmed.*

The elder son was not happy at all. He was angry and would not go in.

Don't you think the Pharisees knew to whom Jesus was pointing? The fact that he would not go in showed his prodigality.

Referring to verse 28, *"His father came out and begged the older brother to come in and rejoice with them."* I can almost hear the older brother saying, "It will not last. It won't be two weeks until he will be back again. He is rotten and humanity does not change. He has always been like this. Mark my words, it won't last." When people make these kinds of remarks, they are really saying that they hope the situation fails again-- they are predicting and looking forward to it.

According to the culture of that day, the elder son was go to in immediately and be a gracious host, but instead he stood outside complaining he had never had a party on his behalf.

He said, "All these years I have worked hard for you and never once refused to do a single thing you told me to do, and in all that time, you never gave me one young goat for a feast with my friends." (He really was having a pity party.)

Does this sound like something you or I have said at one time or another, such as…I'm a hard worker and what do I get for it? Nothing. They never tell me when I do well, only when I goof. And they always speak to me in scorn and a self-righteous spirit."

Verse 30: "Yet, when this son of yours comes back after spending your money (I'm sure he wanted to say, our money) on prostitutes, you celebrate by killing the finest calf we have on the place."

The father should never have gone out to talk to him. He should have sent a servant to bid him come. This father threw all culture aside and entreated him like he did the younger son. He had the love of the Heavenly Father in him. This is what Jesus was showing the Pharisees—that they gave more attention to the laws of the land, than the true law of God.

Let's pull out some scriptures that reveal the spirit of the Pharisees.

John 9:13 *"Then they took the man (former blind man) to the Pharisees." Now as it happened this all occurred on the Sabbath. As they question him, they find that Jesus made some mud by spitting on the clay ground. He picked it up, smoothed it out, and put it on the blind man's eyes—then told him to go wash in the pool of Siloam. Siloam means sent. The water of this pool did not originate there, but came from another source.* God's love does not originate in me, but is sent from the Heavenly Father because of Jesus' finished work on the cross. He entered the Holy of Holies of Heaven and completed the covering for my sin, and then was asked by His father to come and sit on His right side. The reason we know this is because the Holy Ghost Fire came down on the day of Pentecost, and licked up the *120's sin out of their lives.* They were filled with God's Love and Spirit whereby they laid their life on the line for God's work and glory. **(GOD IS SENDING HIS PRECIOUS SPIRIT THROUGH ME NOW. I FEEL IT!)**

Back to the Pharisees in John 9:15, *"Then they asked him all about his healing and he told them how it happened. Some of them said, this man is not from God because he is working on the Sabbath. Now the man*

113

that was healed said, "I think he is a prophet sent from God." The Pharisees said, "This is just another fake healing. Let's go talk to his parents."

But his parents answered, "Yes, he is our son, but he is of age, ask him." When the healed man told them again, he added, "Do you want to be disciples, too? They cursed him and said, "You are his disciple, but we are disciples of Moses. We know God has spoken to Moses, but as for this fellow, we don't know anything about him."

I think you get the picture; they did not have a spirit of love. This was the same kind of spirit the elder son manifested.

We see the revelation of the father's love for the elder son in verse 31. *"Look, dear son," his father said to him, "You and I are very close. Everything I have is yours."*

Catch the vision—everything the father has is ours through Christ. It is right to celebrate. For He is your brother. He was dead and has come back to life! HE WAS LOST AND IS FOUND.

The fact that the elder son would not go in and embrace his younger brother with a true spirit of forgiveness and take up his place as the host of the celebration feast, proves that he did not honor and respect his father. Nor did he love his brother, and wished he had died in the far country where he spent all his inheritance. He not only had a hateful spirit, but also a proud one that says, *"I'm glad I am not like you, but rather a good performer and full of good works."*

Back up to verse 28: *"But he was angry and not willing to go in."* The elder son cared nothing for his brother. In this respect he served to illustrate the indifference of the Scribes and the Pharisees to their openly sinful, vicious spirit.

The elder son was disgracing his father in almost the same degree the younger son did—by becoming angry and refusing to go in the house.

Jesus doesn't leave any room for the Pharisees to wonder or doubt whom the elder brother represents in the parable. They were not celebrating or being joyful when the gentiles and publicans were coming into the house of God, receiving salvation, and enjoying full son-ship status.

There is a strong lesson on the teaching of salvation by grace and grace alone in this parable. When the younger son had spent all and came back home, he knew he was nothing and had nothing to offer but his trust in his father. *"For by grace are you saved through faith, and that not of yourself, for we are his workmanship created in Christ Jesus unto good works, which God has ordained before that we should walk in them."*

The elder son was working his way, or trying to work, his way into the inheritance rather than just receiving it.

Verse 32: It was necessary, it was proper, the right thing to do. Had the elder brother been right, he would have rejoiced at the return of his prodigal, but now, repentant brother. If the Scribes and Pharisees had been in a proper state of mind and heart, they would have rejoiced at the Savior's efforts to save even the worst men and women from eternal damnation and eternity without God.

Jesus' description of the father's response and love for the two sons teaches several important truths:

1) God has compassion for the lost because of their horrible state of being.

2) God loves them so much that He never stops grieving over them and continues to wait for their return.

3) When sinners see their true state of slavery to sin and separation from God, and sincerely turn to Him, He is more than ready to receive them "with forgiveness, love, compassion, grace and the power to become sons of God." The benefits of Christ's death, the Holy Spirit's influence, and God's rich grace are all made available to those who seek Him.

4) God's joy over the return of sinners is immeasurable.

Verse 10)...*In the same way, I tell you there is rejoicing in the presence of the angels of God over one sinner who repents.*

YES, GOD REALLY LOVES YOU AND ME!

"Jesus came as High Priest of this better system which we now have. He went into that greater, perfect tabernacle in heaven, not made by men nor part of this world, AND ONCE AND FOR ALL, took blood into that inner room, the Holy of Holies, and sprinkled it on the mercy seat, but it was not the blood of goats and calves. No, He took His own blood and with it He, by Himself, made sure of our eternal salvation. (Hebrews 9:11-12)

Now that we have the key scripture for this subject, let's go to St. John 14:1-3, where Jesus is revealing to His followers how much He loves them, by His plans for them.

John 14:1-3 *"Let not your heart be troubled. You are trusting God, now trust in Me. There are many homes up there where My Father lives, and I am going to prepare them for your coming. When everything is ready, then I will come and get you, so that you can always be with Me where I am. If this were not so, I would tell you plainly."*

"I am telling you these things now while I am still with you. But when the Father sends the Comforter instead of me, and by the Comforter, I mean the Holy Spirit; He will teach you very much, as well as remind you of everything I myself have told you. I am leaving you with a gift – peace of mind

121

and heart! The peace I give isn't fragile like the peace the world gives. So let not our hearts be troubled, and neither let it be afraid. (John 14:25-27)

Two things Jesus speaks of here: PEACE AND THE HOLY SPIRIT. Remember these two things: Peace and the Holy Spirit. The second part of verse 27, sounds like verse one. *"Let not your hearts be troubled."* John 14:28 *"Remember what I told you. I am going away."(*v16)

"Mary," Jesus said. She turned toward Him. *"Master!"* she exclaimed. In verse 14, Mary did not know it was Jesus. Now that is very strange, because she traveled with Jesus and his disciples the majority of his earthly ministry. (Luke 8:2) She traveled

with him for about three years and didn't recognize him.

In verse 17, *"Don't touch Me,"* he cautioned, *"For I have not yet ascended to the Father. But go find my brothers and tell them that I ascend to my Father and your Father, My God and your God."* Jesus said to Mary, *"Don't touch Me!" For I have not yet ascended."* If he had not yet ascended, then where had He been?

In Ephesians 4:9-10, the word, He ascended, what does it mean, but that he also descended into the lower parts of earth? (v10). He who descended is Himself; also the One Who ascended far above all the heavens, that He might fulfill all things." Go back to verse 8, it is quite interesting.

"Having ascended on high, He led captivity captive and gave gifts unto men." He conquered all His foes, and led a multitude of captives as He rose from the grave. In the book of 1 Peter 3:19, *"He preached to the spirits in prison."* Living Bible, vs 19. *"And it was in the spirit that he visited the spirits in prison, and preached to them."*

To understand more fully why Jesus said to Mary Magdalene, *"Touch Me not,"* because He had not yet ascended to the Holy of Holies to present His own blood for the sins of mankind ONCE AND FOR ALL. The presumption is, soon after He first saw Mary Magdalene, He ascended to His Father and then returned to instruct His disciples further, to give them opportunities for touching Him and examining His wounds, as is shown further on in this chapter.

Remember: Peace and the Holy Spirit. (John 20:18-19) Mary told the disciples, she had seen the Lord. Then the same day at evening, (where had Jesus been all day?) Could He have ascended to His Father? Could He have fulfilled all things? He said, *"I am going away and I am coming back. I am going to the Father, so you can have a relationship with Him through Me, for I will send the Holy Spirit. (What glory, joy and expectation are building up in my spirit as I write these words! Oh think that His Spirit can indwell my spirit, glory-glory-glory-hallelujah! I am his child for evermore!)*

To Mary, he said, "Don't touch Me," Because He had not yet ascended, but when he saw Thomas, who was not there with the other disciples, but was now present, who had said, *"If I can see and touch Him, I will believe."* So when He saw Thomas, He said, *"Touch Me, put your hand in My side and touch Me."* (John 20.24-27) Because at this time Jesus had ascended to the Father and returned to strengthen the disciples and remind them of the promise of the Holy Spirit upon them.

A little side note: How did Thomas know about Jesus' hands and His side? He was either at the cross when Jesus was crucified or he had heard of it from an eye witness. *"Touch me,"* He said to Thomas, and He is also saying to you and me, *'Touch Me."* I desire with all my heart to be touching Him all the time. (Ephesians 4:9) Now when He descended into the lower parts of the earth, He preached to the Old Testament saints, and led captivity captive. (Eph 4:8)

Some teachers of the Word think the Old Testament saints were in a holding pattern, called Abraham's bosom. Now when Jesus spoke to one of the men being crucified with him, the one who said, "Jesus, remember me when Thou comest into Thy Kingdom." Jesus answered him back, *"Today you shall be with Me in Paradise."* Now, this much we know, that Jesus led the Old Testament saints from a holding place

127

(Abraham's bosom), to a place called paradise where they are waiting for the trumpet to sound that we all may be called up together for the great wedding of heaven.

(Luke 24:51) *"And it came to pass, that, while He was blessing them, He parted from them and was borne up into Heaven."*

Ephesians 4:8 Teaches: *"The gifts received by the ascended Savior, he bestows upon men."* (v9) Notice that it says, *"He returned to heaven."* This means, He had first come down to earth, even to the lowest parts, before He could return to heaven.

In Matthew 27:50, the account is given of the happenings that took place when Jesus dismissed His Spirit and died. *"And Jesus, crying again with a loud voice, yielded up His Spirit. (v51) And behold the veil of the temple was rent in two, from top to bottom; and the earth was shaken, and the rocks were rent (split) (vs52). And the tombs were opened; and many bodies of the saints who had fallen asleep were raised. (v53) And coming forth out of the tombs after His resurrection, they entered into the Holy City, and appeared to many."*

Let us put these things into our own words. After the resurrection, Jesus descended to the lower parts of the earth, and said to Satan, "Give Me the keys that unlock the doors to all of these Old Testament saints."

When the doors were opened, and all the saints walked out, Jesus said, "Come on children, we are going to the Father." Once on their way, Jesus also said, "I have got to stop by earth and give Mary some instructions to tell my disciples, so they will remember and believe."

The Old Testament saints then requested of Jesus, "While you are talking to Mary, would you mind if we walked around Jerusalem?" It really got exciting! Isaiah, Jeremiah, Daniel, etc. introduced themselves to some of the citizens of that day, and they could hardly believe it.

After that day of so much excitement, I can see in my spirit, Jesus leading the Old Testament saints onto Glory, and as they arrived at the gates of Paradise, they began to shout with a mighty voice, *"Lift up your heads, Oh ye gates, and be lifted up you everlasting doors, that the King of Glory may come in."* (Ps 27:7-10)   And the Guardians of Heaven said, *"Who is the King of Glory?"* And they answered, *"The Lord strong in battle, the Lord mighty in battle is He."* Then the gates opened and the King of Glory went in. Now this was the first day of the week. What had Jesus been doing in this time? Why did He tell Mary, "I've got to go." What did He do when he left Mary? What took Him all day? Why did she not recognize Him? What was different about His appearance?

Turn to Hebrews 9: What did He do? Where did He go? We know he went to the

Father, but what did He specifically do while he was there?

(Hebrews 9:12) *He sprinkled His own blood in the most holy place in heaven.* The pattern God gave Moses to build on earth was a copy of the one in Heaven. There is a real most Holy Place in Heaven and a real High Priest. The High Priest of Heaven has ONCE AND FOR ALL entered into the Most Holy Place and sprinkled his blood on the Mercy Seat. V13) Jesus, the Son of God, offered Himself without spot to His Father God. How much more should that blood purge your conscience from dead works to serve the Living God? The old sacrifices could not purge your conscience.

(Hebrews 10:1-3) *If the blood of calves and goats could have cleansed the sins of the people and conscience, (vs2) else would they not have ceased to be offered? Because the worshipers, having been cleansed once and for all, would have no more conscience of sins.* (v3) *But in these sacrifices there is a remembrance of sins year by year.* (v4) *For it is impossible that the blood of bulls and goats should take away sins.* (V5)

Wherefore coming into the world, He saith, "Sacrifice and offering thou did not wish but a body didst thou prepare for Me; in whole burnt offerings and sacrifices for sin thou hast no pleasure." Then said, "Lo, I come, in the volume of the book it has been written concerning Me, to do thou will, Oh God."

Saying above, sacrifices and offerings for sin, Thou didst not wish, neither has pleasure there in, which indeed, are offered according to the law, then has he said, "Lo I have come to do Thy will."

"He taketh away the first that He may establish the second, in which we have been sanctified through the offering of the body of Jesus Christ ONCE AND FOR ALL."

Now, let's go back to Chapter 9:18, *"Wherefore, not even the first covenant has been dedicated without blood; for when every commandment had been spoken by Moses to all the people according to the law, taking the blood of the calves and of the goats, with water and scarlet wool and hyssop, He sprinkled both the book itself and all the people, saying, 'This is the blood of the covenant which God commanded in respect to you.' Moreover, the tabernacle and all the vessels of the service, He sprinkled in like manner with the blood."*

WHAT ARE THE VESSELS TODAY IN THE CHURCH? (2 Cor. 4:7) *"But we have this treasure in earthen vessels, which the exceeding greatness may be of God and not from ourselves."*

THIS TREASURE IN EARTHERN VESSELS; IN HUMAN BODIES, CHRIST WAS MOST DEFINITELY THE VESSEL OF GOD. HE, CHRIST, IS OUR EXAMPLE.

135

JOHN 13:15 *"For I gave you an example, that, as I did to you, you also should do."* In other words, He said, *"I have given you an example to follow."*

He was instructing them to minister to one another in whatever way they needed to. Don't seek the high places, but rather, what God, the Father wills you to do.

In 2 Timothy 4:12, He, the Holy Spirit, is telling Christians to become an example or model, to other believers for them to follow, in speech, in conduct in love, in faith and in purity. (I Peter 2:21) *"Christ who suffered for you is your example. Follow in His steps. He never sinned, never told a lie, never answered back when insulted, when he suffered, He did not threaten to get even.*

He left His case in the hands of His Father God.

NOW, LET'S GO BACK TO THE PURGING OF SIN—Christ offered a better sacrifice to God with His own blood than the Priest could with the blood of bulls and goats, which was not his own, which was only a pattern or type of the offering of Christ own blood of the holy of Holies in heaven.

Hebrews 9:24: *For Christ entered not into holy places made with hands, pattern of the time, but in heaven itself, now to appear in the presence of God in our behalf,* (vs25) *Not yet that He should many times offer Himself as the high priest enters into the Holy of Holies every year with blood of His own.* (v26) *But now, ONCE AND FOR ALL, at the end of the ages, He Christ, has been manifested for the putting away of sin through the sacrifice of Himself.* (vs27) *And in as much as it is appointed to men once to die."*

ONCE TO DIE, WHY MUST WE DIE? Because Eve and Adam ate of the forbidden fruit? The real reason was disobedience, which is a neglect or refusal to obey. To obey is to follow the command or guidance of, to comply with.

Genesis 3:1 *"The serpent said to the woman, "You mean God won't let you eat any of this beautiful fruit in this magnificent garden? Why woman, you are the splendid grandeur of beauty and the fruit of this* garden will only add to it, therefore, I am sure God will let you eat of it, so you can be more beautiful. You must have misunderstood what God really said." Now he, the serpent, has her thinking, and she will now turn to talking with him. Jesus said, *"Let your yes be yes and your no be no. For any more than this is of the evil one."*

Remember what the serpent said, "Are you telling me that God won't let you eat any of this lovely, beautiful fruit?"

"Of course we may eat it," the *woman said, "It is only the fruit from the tree in the center of the garden that we are not to partake of. God said, we are not to eat it or even touch it, or we will die."* (v4). Then, the old serpent hissed, *"That's a lie,*

you will not surely die. (v5) God knows that when you eat of the tree of knowledge, you will become like Him and your eyes will be opened. You will know good from evil like he does, but you will not surely die."

LISTEN TO THE HALF TRUTHS AND LIES SATAN PUT TO HER. (V6) THE WOMAN WAS CONVINCED THAT SHE COULD USE THIS KNOWLEDGE FOR GOD AND HIS GLORY. I CAN IMAGINE ALL KINDS OF THINGS HERE THAT SHE THOUGHT. HERE IS ONE OF THEM:

With this added knowledge and my deeper understanding being opened in knowing and distinguishing good from evil, I would be a better helpmate to Adam, whom I love with all my heart and we could better serve God.

Now she has completely forgotten the command of God of which she at one time fully understood. And you know what happens next; *she ate some of the forbidden fruit and then offered some to her husband; which he also did eat.* (v7) *And as they ate this forbidden fruit they became aware of their nakedness and were so embarrassed they somehow put fig leaves together to cover their nakedness. (v8) So, that evening the beginning of the next day, they heard the sound of God walking in the garden.*

WOULDN'T YOU LIKE TO KNOW WHAT IT SOUNDED LIKE? WELL YOU CAN. IT CAN BE THE SOUND OF A

SLIGHT BREEZE OR A ROARING WATERFALL AND IT MOVES WHERE HE PLEASES. (John 3:8)

Sometimes the breathing of the Spirit is as gentle as in 1 Samuel 3:3 while little Samuel was sleeping in the temple near the Ark. The Lord called, "Samuel, Samuel."

"Yes", Samuel replied, "What is it?" He jumped up and ran to Eli, "Here I am, what do you want?" Of course, it was God calling him, not Eli. So the fourth time God called to Samuel he said, "Yes, Lord, I am listening."

OH, THAT SPEAKS TO ME, "YES, LORD, I AM LISTENING."

THE STRONGEST WIND FOR MAN TO BE AFFECTED BY WAS THE WIND

OF THE HOLY SPIRIT ON THE DAY OF PENTECOST. IT IS STILL BLOWING TODAY WHERE IT PASSES.

A good example of this wind blowing in strength, power and great sound is found in Acts 9:3: *"As Paul was nearing Damascus, suddenly a brilliant light from heaven shown directly upon him.* (v4) *He fell to the ground and heard a voice saying to him, "Saul, Saul, why are you persecuting me?"*

"Who is speaking?" (THE LIGHT AND VOICE WERE SO STRONG) *Saul pleaded, tell me sir, and I will listen."* *And the voice replied, "I am Jesus, the one you are persecuting.* (v6) *Now get up and go into the city and wait for my instruction."*(V7) *The voice was so strong that the men with*

Saul heard it, but saw no man. (v8) The light blinded Saul and the mighty voice demanded his attention. (V10) **"Now, listen up, let this capture your spirit.**

In John 3:8, it is just the experience that every truly converted person presumably has. The Holy Spirit breathes upon the sinner, and awakens in him a sense of his sins. Then as the repentant sinner looks to Christ, the spirit breathes into him spiritual life and he becomes a new creature in Christ Jesus.

NOW LET'S GO BACK TO HEBREWS 9:27. *"For it is appointed unto men once to die; the one death of the redeemed, accords with the one death of the*

Redeemer." (V28) *"To bear the sins of many. To bear away all the sins of all who accept Him and put them away by His own sacrifice in their behalf. Those who are eagerly waiting for Him, waiting for His 2nd coming. Without sin, without any reference to bearing sin anymore, as He did on the cross, but to give His followers full and everlasting salvation."*

DO YOU REMEMBER HOW YOU FELT WHEN YOU WERE SAVED? DID YOU FEEL LIGHT WHEN YOU SAID, "JESUS COME INTO MY HEART?" The Holy Spirit bore witness with your spirit that the connection was complete.

Romans 8:9 *"You are controlled by your new nature if you have the Spirit of*

God living in you. And if you don't have the Spirit of God living in you, you are not a Christian at all." (v10) *Even though Christ lives in you, your body will die because of sin, but your spirit will live because of your trust in Christ, your sins have been pardoned.* (V11) *And as the Spirit of God, who raised up Jesus from the dead, lives in you, He the Holy Spirit will make your dying body live again after you die.* (V12,13)

The believer is told why he is no longer bound by sin. Brothers and sisters you have made a covenant with Jesus and he has made one with you that is binding on both of our parts and the Holy Spirit is the title company that sees to its performance and helps the believer to carry out his part. The contract with the previous owner, the devil, has been broken and changed completely. The title is now in your hands. So as you, through the Holy Spirit, crush the old sinful nature and its evil deeds, you shall live.

Now you can understand what is meant in v14, *"For all who are led by the Spirit are the sons of God."* V16) "The Holy Spirit speaks to us deep in our hearts and tells us that we really are God's children."

But Brother Herb, what if we sin against God after we have accepted Christ? We shall have the Holy Spirit to lead us out of it. But how?

1 John 2:1, *"We have Jesus to plead for us before the Father." (v2) "Jesus is the forgiveness for our sins." V3) "Let us allow*

the Holy Spirit to look deep within us and to help us to really look on the inside of ourselves, so we will know what He wants us to do."

James 5:15, *"If one has committed sins; sins that led to his sickness, it shall be forgiven him. That is, He will on the exercising of faith, receive forgiveness for his sins. The Lord will raise him up, heal him, and restore him to health. Both healing and forgiveness is the bread from the Lord's table.*

Jesus said both, *"Take up thy bed and walk, thy sins be forgiven thee."* (Matthew 9:5)

NOW CHANGING THE SUBJECT A LITTLE—TO SOWING AND

REAPING. What kind of seeds have you sown in your lifetime? And what kind are you sowing now?

"Whatsoever a man soweth, that shall he also reap." God made this law and God can break it. God said, He will give you the desires of your heart.

God said, *If God through Christ can change spiritual death to spiritual life, then through Christ and God's grace the law of sowing and reaping can be broken. The reaping of bad seed can be broken by the power of God through Christ and the blessed Holy Spirit.*

Watch out Brother Herb, you are trying to change God's laws. No, I am not. I am really teaching the sovereignty of God, He can do what He pleases.

Let's go back to the beginning and pick up the part of the love story that we started with. *"I am going to prepare a place for you, because I want you to be with Me."* Just think, the place is almost ready. I can almost hear the shout, *"The Bridegroom cometh! Go ye out to meet Him! Come away my fair one, I have longed for this moment."* Wouldn't it be wonderful if Jesus would catch his bride away before I finish this page! *"And I shall see him face to face."*

Oh the joy of sin forgiven! Oh the blessings the blood washed know! But let's go back into the field, while it is yet day, for the night is coming when no man can work.

He would that none should perish, but that all would come to repentance.

A story that I heard some time ago proves that our actions speak louder than our words. A prosperous man had a son that was born crippled. After the baby was born, the mother never regained her health and soon died. The father searched for a woman that would care for and love his son. A woman in her early twenties seemed to be very qualified in every way, so she became the boy's nanny. She gave herself so completely to the crippled lad that she denied herself of a normal life of romance and marriage.

After about twenty years of caring for the son, by this time he was a young man, he became very ill and passed away in a brief time. It was almost more than she could bear. A short time later the father who was getting up in years contracted a fatal disease and also died. The attorney came on the appointed day to the huge mansion to read a short, sealed, hand written will to settle the estate. The first instruction was to give the woman that was the son's nanny the first choice of anything inside the house that she wanted. That was all it said. She looked high and low for her favorite piece but always came back to the large picture of the son that hung in the front hall. Finally, she said to the attorney, "I want that picture more than anything else. Yes, I want that picture. I loved him so much that I poured my whole life into his. That boy meant everything to me, give me his picture."

A servant was summoned with a ladder to take down the picture. Upon taking it down and looking on the back, the attorney saw an envelope stapled to it, which he opened and read to himself. Then with great excitement, he read out loud, "The person that loves this picture would also love my son, so I bequeath my entire estate to them."

So it is that those who pour their life into the life and love of God's son will reap everlasting joy, peace and life in the mansion that he has gone to prepare for us. Let us say, "'ONCE AND FOR ALL' I am a believer."

After reading the scriptures and comments in this paper, only a fool would turn away and refuse to believe in and walk with God and his pattern for their life. But there are many that have let the struggles and cares of this life choke out God's word and spirit. Please accept God's prepared place for you. Don't say like the fool, *"Oh I will when I get this or that in life."* (Luke 12:20) *"But God said to him, fool tonight you die. Then who will get it all?"* (v21) Yes every man is a fool who gets rich on earth, but not in heaven.

As a believer, we receive benefits of His sacrifice on the cross and the presenting of His own blood in the Holy of Holies in heaven for the redemption of all mankind that Adam lost in the garden.

Hebrews 10:10: *"By the will of Christ, He offered His body as a sacrifice back there when Mary didn't recognize him. He was on his way to be offered in the holy place. What the earthly priest could not do, Jesus could."*

He did it, ONCE AND FOR ALL THAT I MIGHT BE SAVED once and for all, throughout eternity. Thank you, Father God, for your everlasting Covenant.

There is a Song which says, "He took my sins away. He took them all away, and keeps me singing every day."

Healed Through Prayer
And Parents' Love

~Dr. Peggy A. Buckner

When our daughter Nancy was born, she was diagnosed with having Goldenhar Syndrome. Symptomatic of the disease, she had tumors on both eyes greatly hindering her sight. Her joints were not formed properly. She was also diagnosed as having scoliosis.

After many doctors' visits, and even more tests, we were given the grim prognosis. She would be a vegetable. She would never have a normal childhood. She would be paralyzed, or at best she was to be mentally retarded...severely impaired.

We were in shock, but we knew enough to call on the name of the Lord. The doctors designed a body brace to help her stay in a position to facilitate growth of joints.

Every day we exercised her arms and legs, and stood on God's Word. We still went to visit the doctors, who gave us no hope, but our hope was not in them. Our hope was in Jesus Christ.

We kept working with her. As she grew, the body brace had to be changed. Intermittently, we would take her out of her brace and put her on the floor. We would move her legs and arms as if she were crawling. At about 10 months, she was crawling on her own – not very well, but she could move on her own.

At one year, we had her up teaching her how to walk. Rather than walking, when she got her balance she went to running. At the age of three, we put her in her first race. She came in first place out of 25 other children in her category! Praise God!

At the age of five years, she had surgery on both eyes. She wears eyeglasses, but can see very well. She graduated from high school and college **with honors!** Today she is a beautiful woman working hard in a Christian-based non-profit agency "changing the lives of children" as she puts it. To God be the glory!

✺✺✺✺✺

Child Brought Back To Life

~Wanda Jones

Wanda Jones is the mother of Charlotte Heilaman, a member of The Oaks Fellowship in Red Oak, Texas. (This is Charlotte's description of her mother.) "She is 82, wears high heels, and still cuts her own yard. She is a mighty prayer warrior and people call her to pray all the time. My father passed away when I was 13 and she raised us three girls on Faith because we sure didn't have any money. We didn't really get to participate in extracurricular activities at school because we knew the

159

money just wasn't there. But, God provided our every need and I wouldn't take anything for that lesson. We learned early in life through experience that we could trust Him for anything we needed and it made us strong." The following several testimonials are all from Wanda.

My daughter, Charlotte, and her husband Scott, had purchased a new van and a friend of mine had given me some carpet samples. Charlotte came and we were fixing to go out and pick out some mats for her van.

Before we went out Charlotte saw a skirt of mine and said, "That's pretty." I told her she could have it. She folded it and put it on a chair.

We went to my back yard to get the carpet for her mats. We went through all the samples and just as we loaded them back in the shed I heard a scream. I said, "Oh, no! Some kid has gotten run over!"

We went to the front yard and someone said, "Call an ambulance Jimmie has run over his daughter!"

Heather was about three years old. Charlotte and I ran over there and began praying in tongues. Her daddy, Jimmy, had his arms out holding her. He was staring into space. She was not breathing and I believe she was dead. We kept praying. I held her and was going to kiss her and she started crying!

The ambulance came and took her to Parkland. At Parkland the doctors said she had to have bad broken bones and head injuries.

Her grandmother came and when she got there she was so upset because Heather's mother had on shorts. The grandmother's sister had just given her a dress. She sent her husband out to get the dress for her daughter to put on.

Back at home they had called a prayer meeting at the church and a friend had come to my house that lived out of town. She had on blue jeans and she wanted to go to the prayer meeting. I gave her the skirt I had given Charlotte for her to put on to go the prayer meeting. We stayed all night praying at the hospital. The next morning they said there were no head injuries or even broken bones!

I believe she was dead and God brought her back to life because we prayed, and He healed the head injuries and broken bones! That is not all the story.

The neighbor's son in law was the one that had put Heather in her dad's arms. He was an atheist. His name was John and he sat on my front porch all night. The next morning he told his mother in law that as he stood there with Charlotte and me praying in tongues; and God healed that baby, it made a believer out of him! He got saved that night and later became a Spirit filled Sunday School teacher!

I put the part in about the skirt and the dress to tell how God arranged clothing for them. He is always one step ahead of us!

*****

Judy, who is the mother of Heather, showed us in a current picture on Facebook that Heather is now a beautiful, perfect mother at 29 and has a beautiful 9 year old of her own! God is good!

The following story is not just a story of healing but of God's Providence. Doug and his wife were a long distance from doctors and a hospital if God had not been with them.

God Always Knows Where We Are

~Doug Bell

In 1998, my wife and I started for Alaska, and eight days later we crossed the border of Alaska. It was one of the greatest trips I have ever taken. Little did I know I was headed for a heart attack.

165

We pulled into a fuel stop, topped off with fuel and water and dumped our tanks. When I went to pay the attendant said to me, "Why don't you spend the night and leave in the morning? It's free."

We did but when I got up the next morning I was having hard chest pains. I told Cleta to go and call 911. The paramedics were there in about three minutes. They started IV's in both hands and every time my heart would beat it shook my body so hard it felt like it was going to come out of my chest. I could not breathe and I broke out in a cold sweat. I realized that I was dying.

My wife was walking the floor and praying at the top of her voice. Each time she would pass me I tried to get hold of her, but the nurse would pull my hand back. After what seemed like a long time, I got hold of her. I began to tell her, "I love you, but this where we part company. I am dying!"

She pointed her finger in my face and said, "You are not going to die. God just told me so!"

It was like someone had thrown a bucket of hot water on me from the top of my head to the bottom of my feet. I did not know we were 2 ½ blocks from the only Medicare facility within 200 miles.

They flew us on into Fairbanks and the doctor met us at the door. I had already had five shots of Nitro under the tongue and 5 shots of Demarol. The doctor asked me if I had any cuts or abrasions. I asked why and he said, "You are going to bleed." I went out like a light.

The next morning when I woke up my wife was holding my hand. She asked, "Do you know where you are?"

"Yes."

"Do you know what has happened to you?"

"Yes."

"Do you know where our trailer is?"

"Yes."

She said, "Honey, all the clothes I have is what I have on."

We prayed, "Lord, you have people all over the world. Just send us one. I will be glad to pay whatever they want to go and get our rig and park it behind the hospital."

The next day a young lady came bouncing into my room with a big smile and said, "Hello, I am Lonie Miller!"

I said, "Darling, I don't know you."

She said, "But I know <u>you</u>."

Her sister home schooled with my daughter in law from Dallas, Texas. I gave her my keys and the next day the truck and trailer were sitting behind the hospital!

Six days later they gave me a stress test, and I had another heart attack from the second test. The doctor sent me to Anchorage because the doctor I was supposed to have fallen off his cycle and broke his leg. A trainee took me and did tests. That evening he came to see me and said, "You have done some bad damage to your heart. There's nothing I can do. I am going to medicate you and send you home."

I said, "No! I want to see my doctor."

The next morning a man came into my room on crutches. I asked, "Who are you?"

"I am Doctor Peterson, your doctor." He did one test lying flat on the table. I remember I was very cold. The nurse asked did I get to fish and I said, "No."

That day the doctor did surgery on me and the next day he released me! The nurse brought us two big socks of Salmon and Halibut.

God met every need we had. The nurse at the hospital told us if we had crossed the border into the Yukon there would not have been a doctor for a thousand miles! God ordains every step we take!

How I Came To Know The Lord

~Tayo Lancaster

At the age of 17 I lived in Jackson, Tennessee. A girl I wanted to go out with asked me to come and go to a revival with her. I went and listened to Ken Hall preach, and he was having a healing line.

A man came up in a wheelchair with a deformed leg. The knee was completely out of joint and the foot was turned almost backward. I was very interested to see what God was going to do for something so miraculous. I even told the Lord, "If you will heal that man's leg I will give my heart to you and serve you."

They prayed for the man and, as I watched, the knee went back into place, the foot straightened, and God miraculously healed him! I said to the Lord, "That is good enough for me! Where do I sign?"

I gave my heart to God that night and ever since I have had a special anointing to pray for people with leg problems. I have prayed and God has lengthened legs on the spot. I prayed for one woman to have her leg lengthened and I was holding the wrong leg. She called out, "I don't want to be taller!" So, I prayed again and God made both legs the same.

Even in our Full Gospel Men's Group, I have been privileged to pray for one man which had an injury which left one leg shorter than the other and his pelvis out of adjustment which caused him great pain. God healed Bob Gibson and he has started back to walking and jogging and has not felt pain in his leg and pelvis since we prayed for him!

Back in Jackson, I later wanted to ask Ken Hall to come and have a little Bible study in my home. I had been thinking about asking him and I stopped at the four way stop where one way went to his house and one way continued on to mine. While I was praying for what to do I opened my eyes and I was sitting in his front driveway! I do not know how I got there! Not only that, he was coming out the door with two cups of coffee! He had been told by the Lord I was coming!

We sat on his front porch and made plans to start a Bible study in my home. We grew, and went to a small shopping center location. Then later a man gave him 25 acres along with some money, and he built a church. Today there is a good sized Church which started from the little Bible study in my home!

Blind Baby Healed
~Reverend Sam Farina

In 1996 I experienced a very unexpected miracle. On July 3 my father died and it was a very dark time of sorrow in my life. As I was leaving the hospital after his death, the pastor of First Assembly in Appleton called my cell phone. He insisted that I was to come to his church the next week to speak. As one can imagine, I was low in emotion after the death of my father and the funeral, but decided to go to the church for the multi day meeting.

Only a few minutes into the first

meeting a couple came forward with their baby boy who had recently been diagnosed as blind with no hope for a medical solution. They were holding the medical document from the doctors. I prayed for the baby boy. A week later the couple returned to the meeting holding the boy and a NEW medical document. They had noticed that the baby was tracking their movement after we prayed and decided to take the boy back to the doctor. Once there, the doctors declared that sight had been restored to the child.

I visited with the family two years ago and the boy still had perfect sight!

God Met A Financial Need
~DaLoma Horne

Early on in our marriage, my husband and I had an unexpected bill come up for 150 dollars. It might have been medicine for the kids, or car repair. Whatever it was, it was important to us.

We knelt in our bedroom by the bed and started praying for God to help us find the money. There was a knock on the door, and I told my husband to keep on praying and I would answer the door.

It was an old friend I had not seen in ten years. She handed me a check and said, "I was passing through Lubbock and God told me to look you up in the phone book and give you a check for 150 dollars!" She hugged me and left.

I took the check and knelt by the bed and my husband. I slipped the check under his folded hands, he looked down, and tears came into his eyes. He looked at me in wonder, and I just nodded yes as we both cried.

It is important to note God had the answer on the way before we ever prayed! I have never seen her since!

Answers To Prayers In Sunday School Class

In 1985 my wife and I were co-teaching a Sunday School class in Slaton, Texas, which is just outside of Lubbock. I was the Assistant Manager of the Anthony's Department Store, and my wife was a kindergarten teacher.

We were teaching a unit on "Answers to Prayer." We went over Biblical references to answered prayer, and I also used other reference books for how to pray and ask God to answer.

At the end of the series of lessons I asked the group of adults, "If you knew you had the ear of God, you were in His presence, and you could have anything you want for what would you ask?"

I went around the room, and, when we thought about what we would actually and honestly desire from God if we were to stand in His presence, there was a universal answer. We all said we wanted more of God and to know His ways. We found it interesting not one of us would ask for needs outside of the Spiritual Realm!

One couple had been praying about a son living in Dallas who was away from the Lord. Another couple was having marital problems. A woman named Helen Lee wanted to receive the Baptism of the Holy Spirit with the evidence of speaking in tongues. I wanted direction in my job for I had an offer in another town. None of us would have asked God for the answer to those needs. We would have asked for more of Him.

I told the class, "Then let's just praise God before we go out to the main service. Don't ask Him for anything, but just praise Him as if we had already received the answer." We praised Him for a few minutes, and then went out of our room to the main service.

It was the order of service in that church to have prayer at the altar before the church service began. Our little group went to the altar and began praying. I felt a direction from the Lord to lay hands on Helen Lee and help her pray for the Baptism. She had been seeking earnestly for over 20 years. As soon as I laid my hands on her, she raised her arms and hands and started speaking in tongues for the first time in her life! She died not long after receiving the baptism, but she died knowing God had answered her prayers!

The next Sunday, the couple with the wayward son, told us as they entered their home from church, the telephone was ringing, and it was their son who wanted them to know he went to church that morning and gave his heart to the Lord! The couple having marital problems was holding hands, giggling, and telling us they were to leave on a cruise the next week! Although it meant a move to Lubbock, I worked for another store, and it was a great job until the company was bought out and closed. The direction I was seeking sent us to Houston where all three children received the Holy Spirit Baptism, graduated from the same high school, and went to college together. The three of them graduated from Southwestern Assemblies of God University (SAGU) in Waxahachie, Texas. They are married, and we all now live close to one another in the Dallas area. God answered our prayers and our needs when we sought Him in praise!

Stones About Never Giving Up On Your Kids

As stated above we moved to Katy, Texas, a suburb of Houston, when the kids were in high school. We found a great church which is now named Family Life Assembly of God. It did not take long to find a place for each of us to work in the church. My wife and I began as leaders of the youth, and our kids were involved with the youth. When the church hired a youth pastor, we started teaching a Sunday School class. It was bliss.

I believed my three children were doing great. They were active in the youth group, prayed at the altar, and I thought we had it made. I never realized the power of "peer pressure."

My first indication was my youngest two were letting their grades drop. I felt it was the process of a new school and adjusting to a much larger and difficult curriculum than the small town where they had been. They went to parties on the weekends with other church kids and members of the "A" list. I still was not feeling anything negative, except I did gripe a little about them coming home smelling of cigarette smoke. My wife, however, had much more intuition. The horrible parents we were my wife would go through the girl's purse. She never found cigarettes, but did find disposable cigarette lighters, which she would throw away.

Years later, long after she quit smoking, the daughter laughed about how she could not figure out how she was losing so many lighters. We started paying attention to her friends and how the ones closest to her were a little more "unkempt" than the others who were from church. They had longer hair and shorter dresses, and were trying to get her to spend the night on the weekends. It all came to a head when we got "the call."

She had been driving her car and got stopped for "unsafe backing" from a driveway at 10 pm at night by a cop car a block away. That was enough for the cops to stop her. They searched the car and found a few joints stuffed into the passenger's door pocket. She and her friend had just picked up her friend's boyfriend, a known drug pusher. The police had the house under surveillance, and took all three to the local police station, impounded her car, and put her in jail which prompted "the call". You may know the one. Your child is in trouble.

The phone rang at about 11:30 pm, and it was my daughter crying that she was in jail. She needed 500 dollars for bail. After going from surprise to disbelief, I was angry. Where had we missed it? We had done everything right. Church was a part of her life since birth. She had always been so sensitive and cried in nearly every service. I am sure now she was under conviction for what she was doing.

I called and got my pastor out of bed, bless his heart, and he went to an ATM in the middle of the night to get part of the bail money. In the meantime, the police had taken her and her female friend from the satellite station to the main police station in downtown Houston. That is where we had to go and pay her bail. We were informed she would not be released until 11:00 am. We ate a little then went and waited at the police station for several hours.

I watched people come and go and I was hurting to think my daughter was just like them. She did not belong there in my mind. I was trying to decide if I would use my belt on her (probably not), move her to a convent, lock her in her room until she turned 30, and several more scenarios. At the least she was going to hear me raise my voice, as if yelling at her would do any good.

We were standing on the sidewalk in downtown where they let out the prisoners when my daughter came out. Surprisingly, there was not a lot of drama. She came up and laid her head on my chest without saying a word. I put my arms around her. Her mother put her arms around both of us. She, her mother, and I all cried.

To her credit that was a turning point in her life. She turned her back on her former friends to the point she would cry but not answer the phone when they called. After a few calls and me asking what they wanted, the phone stopped ringing. I would take her and pick her up after school. The new car we had given her was in my name, and after retrieving it from the impound lot, I took it back to the sales lot. We were not behind on payments, and when I told the credit department why I was bringing it back I left it. The car sold quickly. I never had to make another payment.

She graduated from high school a couple months later and joined her older sister at SAGU. They shared an apartment or two and she met a nice pastor's son, got married, and is doing well.

I have been active in church since I was 11 years old. I was filled with the Holy

Spirit in college. I have been teaching and praying for others for years. I saw God heal and deliver people. I was too proud of what God had done. I thought my family was untouchable.

My son came to me a couple of months before he was to graduate and said he would not be able to walk across the stage and receive his diploma with his class. He would have to go to summer school for at least one more credit before he could receive his diploma. I prayed and prayed over him and his future. We decided to sign him out of school and go get his GED test for a high school diploma. He had been a good student but his partying on the "A" list had been his undoing. He wanted to be accepted: and he was.

He had excellent grades for 12 years, and he had no problem passing and obtaining his GED. The other kids taunted him with not receiving his diploma, but he pointed out he had his degree before they did. A matter of interest to me was two other parents signed their students out of school at the same time. Obviously the classroom was not teaching our kids what they needed. A friend of mine gave my son a job washing driveways and patios with a high pressure hose and after a few weeks he decided college was a lot less hot and messy. He enrolled at SAGU.

Even at a Christian college with the teachers blessing each class by prayer, and the students having to attend a daily chapel service, they have a way of finding others of like interests, i.e. users of alcohol and drugs. It culminated with me receiving another of "The Call."

My son had been drinking and ran off the road and hit a highway sign. He was in jail. I let him think about what he had been doing and where he was going if he continued. At the price of me agonizing every moment, I let him stay in jail. He had to wait a few days before he was to go before the judge. We were going through town on our way to see my wife's family for Christmas, and we went to visit him.

The visiting room at the jail had a wall of reinforced glass with a hole in it to visit with the prisoners. When my son came out and saw me he put his fist up to the glass. I did also. The "bump" as the kids call it, was when my anger went away. He was a broken boy. The swagger was gone, and he realized Daddy and Mom were right. I held my hand up against his on my side of the glass and we all cried. We had told him often how it **cost** to serve satan, but it **paid** to serve the Lord. A few years later he used the same line in a sermon in front of other young people.

I did not have enough money for his bail, but I called my mother in law and she said she would give it to me.

I went over to the bail bonding office and walked into a room with four rough looking men smoking cigars and playing cards. The leader stood and came around behind the desk when I said I needed to get my son out of jail. He frowned when I said I would bring him the money on my way back through town in a few days. However, unbelievably he let me fill out my son's release forms and he said he would make the call to let him out. We went over to the jail and waited by the outside door. My son had a bag and a Bible with him when he came out. We all hugged and cried again.

My son had always been fairly reticent to talk with us about what he felt and what was going on in his life. Possibly it was because he did not want to give away his wrong doing. However, he talked nonstop the entire 5 hour trip to Lubbock from Waxahachie. We smiled at one another behind his back but we let him talk.

He told us about a preacher offering him a Bible and my son took it and started reading intently for the first time. He told me he kept finding verses that I had told him. He had been praying furiously after seeing us we could get him out.

One of the other inmates saw something in my son and he told him, "This ain't no place for you. We all may belong in here, but you get out and don't come back!"

We went and had a great Christmas, and I came back with 500.00 in cash for the bondsman. He told me after we left they looked at one another and said, "What just happened? Did we let a prisoner walk on just someone's signature? We usually require everything from car titles to house deeds as collateral, but you came in here and walked out with your son. That never happens!"

I was thinking it was an answer to prayer, but I am sure he sensed it too. He just shook his head as if he still could not believe it. "I must be slipping," he said. Maybe I ought to have explained it to him, but those were not my people. The less time I had to remain in his cigar smoke filled office the better I liked it.

At my son's trial a few days later, before the sternest judge I have ever seen, I stood beside my son as he told him he was going to make an example out of another church kid. He fined him plus gave him 1200 hours of community service. He sneered and told him he would be back in his court. I was proud of my son as he stood straight and said, "No sir, you won't!" He didn't.

I was called to jury duty a few years later after we moved to Red Oak in the judge's court and he remembered me and my son. I was happy to tell him he had become a good man and now had a Master's Degree with a beautiful wife and daughter. He is an assistant principal in a high school, and has given his testimony several times in front of hundreds of at risk students. It was a pleasure to see that old judge confess to me with tears in his eyes he was glad, because he too could see the potential in my son.

A few weeks later after his release, during a revival in Katy by a Spirit-filled evangelist by the name of Chris D'Amico, my son was baptized in the Holy Spirit, and he and his best friend lay on their back speaking in tongues with their arms raised for over two hours! The church and my wife and me went home and closed the doors which locked automatically. We knew they were in Good Hands and we wanted him to get a "double dose infilling" of the Spirit. Later, my son said he never knew it was dark until he came to himself. He had been seeing a Heavenly light.

Don't give up praying for your kids and family. Satan is a merciless and unforgiving enemy and he wants to destroy them. However, praise the Lord, we serve a God in heaven who sent His son to give you and them mercy and to forgive them of their sins.

My son thanked me later for not giving up on him, but I told him how much I wanted to thank <u>him</u> for I was determined to not stop praying for him and all my kids. The experience drove me to my knees, and I prayed all night several times, took a shower, and went to work the next day. I would do it again.

Although this is a personal "Stone" for me, I want everyone to know what God can do for you and yours too!

~Don Horne

The following is a very special addendum to this book which came my way from a special lady in our Sunday school class, and I am gratefully including it here and in the revised edition of "Red Jacket And Yellow Squash"(a previous book of mine).

~Don Horne, Editor

My Life
~Berna Mae (Robison) Pruett

I grew up in an Assembly of God Minister's Home. I was born in Texas, and I had wonderful parents who loved and served the Lord faithfully. I also lived my growing up years in Texas. I attended Southwestern

Bible Institute in my Junior and Senior years of High School. At Southwestern, I became acquainted with Dick Pruett, who grew up in Corpus Christi, Texas. We were married in November of 1951. We were invited to become an Assistant Pastor in the City of Pampa, Texas and began our Ministry there in January of 1952 at the First Assembly of God Church. In those early years, we ministered in Texas, then our ministry took us to California two different times. Finally, in the late 60's we moved there again and this time stayed 17 years in full time Ministry.

We had a really fine, loving, enjoyable marriage. Dick always treated me so very special. We sang together in church, directed choir, and put together Trio's and Quartets. I played the piano and Dick always included me in the Ministry Pattern. He was a very fine man, husband, father, and was liked by everyone. Ministry was his life and God used him in so many ways. He was an astute preacher of the Word. He could take control well, always had lots of great ideas, and being a director was very natural for him

We have five wonderful children.....four daughters and one son. Now I also have two sons-in-law, and one daughter-in-law. I have eight grandchildren, four grandchildren in-law and two great grandsons. It is a wonderful, close, enjoyable, fun loving family. I couldn't enjoy them more.

This is my Testimony of God's Love and Grace through the years.

In 1976, my husband of 25 years began to have problems with his eye sight caused by his Diabetes condition. In 1979, a few days before his 50th birthday, he woke up one morning and could not see his face in the mirror. This began a whole new way of life for him and for me. For a man always in charge of everything.....this was really a difficult time. Of course, I had to take over responsibilities that had always been his and be sure that he did not feel like a "nobody"! It was a very traumatic time for us both. But God, our wonderful Lord, was always right there to guide and assure us of His presence and control. Dick experienced many conversations with the Lord, and God gave him so many words of encouragement. One of them was, *"Give me the brokenness of your life and I will touch hundreds and even thousands of others who are broken in some area of their life and I will restore them"*.

He was well known in the Southern California Assemblies of God because he had served in the District Office as Christian Education Director. So, when Pastors became aware of his situation, they began to call and ask him to speak to their congregations. They needed his POSITIVE word to their people in need. God gave him a wonderful message of hope and the ability to deliver it without 6 pages of notes, which of course, was a new experience for him.

And, during all these new ways in our lives, I personally sensed the Lord so near to me. In the many times when I really did not know what tomorrow would bring, and actually did not know what the next hour could bring, such a peace flooded over me that could only come from our Lord. At one point when I was feeling troubled, the Lord led me to read a scripture in the Bible. Proverbs, chapter 3, verses 5 & 6:

"Trust in the Lord with all thine heart, and lean not unto thine own understanding. In all thy ways acknowledge Him, and He shall direct thy paths." As I was reading this, He was also giving me a

"tune" that seemed to fit with the words of the scripture. I went to the piano and began to play the notes I was hearing, and then as I added the words I realized that He had actually given me a song to sing! What a wonderful experience! The words of the scripture were guiding me to trust Him and that He was directing me! I did, and I have, and He has never ever failed me.

We were invited to Texas in late 1983 to Minister in various Churches, and upon visiting our 'ol Alma Mater, Southwestern Assemblies of God College, we reconnected with Alumni and Friends of the past. One day after arriving back home in California, we received a phone call from Dr. Dick Guynes, the President of

Southwestern. He and Dick had been students there in the late '40's.

He said, "Dick, the Lord has been talking to me and I feel that you are supposed to be here at Southwestern as our Campus Pastor." What a shock! Asking someone who is blind to be Campus Pastor? Move back to Texas.....leaving our children in California....could this really be the thing to do at this point of our life? Well, we began to have our own conversation with the Lord. We made a trip back to Texas, and felt that it really was the Lord's will for us. So, in May of 1984, we and our son moved to Waxahachie, Texas, to fill the position of Campus Pastor, and our son would attend college. It was a tremendous experience for each of us. The Lord began immediately to use both of us on a daily basis. We made all the arrangements for the Chapel Services each day, and, Dick, as pastor, led the service. We arranged for special music and speakers. I am thankful how the Lord used me also in so many ways in the midst of the greatest trauma of our lives.

I enjoyed all the responsibilities, and the contact with people was such a great blessing. Because Dick needed me to prepare him for each day, the Lord was using me in ways that I had never imagined. Yes, the Lord's strength for me was moment to moment, and He never failed to be there in every situation that would occur.

In Feb of '85, Dick had kidney failure and was placed on dialysis 3 days per week. This was another great responsibility for me, and so difficult for him physically. But he kept going.....never missing a day at the College. November 30th of that year we celebrated our 34th wedding anniversary. Three days later, on December 2nd, Dick woke up that morning saying, "I don't feel good." That was the day that the Lord took him home to Heaven. It was something we had always known could happen, but, it was quite a shock to realize "this was the day."

So, after his Memorial Services and burial, again, my life is taking on another new phase. Yes, I am lonely and miss him so very much, but I am also very comforted to realize that he is now out of pain. He is seeing all his loved ones in Heaven, and enjoying his new home. He knows that the Lord will continue to take care of me. Yes, and He has! God is SO FAITHFUL!

When the College hired us, they had salaried me so that we could keep Dick's disability income. We did not realize at the time that it would be a tremendous help for me when his time would come. So, since I was the employed one, I continued with all our responsibilities each day. I was so glad to have my Son here with me. I was not at home alone. He understood what I was going through, and we had a great relationship. My daughters were also very near me too, even though they were miles away. They were so loving and attentive to my needs, and always there when I needed them.

Of Course, I had many questions about what the future would hold for me without Dick. Like......should I go back to California where my daughters still lived, and where Dick and I had so many personal friends?

Lord, "What does the future hold?" was my greatest question. So, time passed, and the Board met in February and asked me to stay on and continue with the responsibilities that we had been given in the beginning. It was awesome to realize the Lord really was looking after me, as He had promised. This was beyond anything I had ever imagined. This was such a tremendous blessing, to continue to be here where we had been together and enjoy all the students that I meet each year.....WHAT A BLESSING.

That was 26 years ago and I am still employed at Southwestern, now a University. I could not ask for a more wonderful place to be, and to have been, all these years. I have come to know so many students....made friends with Faculty and Staff through the years.....get to hear from and see Alumni I attended Southwestern with. It is the greatest Blessing the Lord could have ever allowed for me to experience. I will never stop praising Him for his faithfulness to me. I realize He had my life planned from the beginning, and each experience was in His Hands to bring me to where I am today. THANK YOU LORD!

I want each of you to know that just as the Lord had my life in His hands all the way.....you too can expect that He is leading and planning your life each day that you serve Him. We can make preparations daily, and should, but God has His plan for us and it is so wonderful to know that HE IS IN CHARGE. Always know whatever your situation is...you can, and must always, *"Trust in the Lord with all your heart and lean not unto thine own understanding. In all thy ways acknowledge Him and He shall direct thy paths."*

So, remain faithful and experience God's blessings on your life. Again I say, "HE IS FAITHFUL!"

Demanded For Trial

"DEMANDED FOR TRIAL" was the final sermon preached by Reverend Richard Pruett, only eight days before his death. This moving sermon/testimony was ministered to the congregation of the Calvary Assembly of God Church, Waco, Texas, during the Sunday evening service, on November 26, 1985.

This special sermon/testimony is dedicated to those going through a time of "trial and testing" in their lives.

I know there is a teaching abroad in our world Christians should not have too many problems; they can confess away their problems, and through confession, everything will be righted...confessing a Cadillac in every garage...just name it and it is yours...it is just a matter of the right confession...the right thought pattern! Anyone who lives beneath that axiom is living beneath his or her privileges, and is walking out of tune with God's will for their lives. BUT, HEAR ME! That is not true to the scriptures, nor is it true to the experience of life.

Jesus said in John's Gospel, chapter 16, *"For in this world ye shall have tribulation but be of good cheer, I have overcome the world."* Sounds like we could have a few problems! And speaking through the lips of James... *"count it all joy when* you fall into divers temptations (tests or trials) knowing this; that the trial of your faith worketh patience, and let patience have her perfect work that you may be mature, wanting nothing."

Yes, it is true we can bring certain circumstances on ourselves, but when our hearts are clean before God and we find ourselves in a valley experience, it is for a purpose. God has something He is working out in our lives. First Peter, chapter 5, verse 10: "After that ye have suffered a while, make you perfect, stablish, strengthen, settle you." So, these are the reasons that difficulties come to us the children of God.

In 1976, I lost the sight in my right eye after having three laser operations performed by one of the finest surgeons in Southern California. Three years later, in 1979, two days after my wife, Berna, and I came home from a vacation in Hawaii, I woke up and could not see anything. I could not see my hand in front of my face. I was later declared legally blind by the State of California. Needless to say, this was very traumatic for me. I despaired for my life, wondering what I was going to do! I had a son to finish raising and get through college. All my hopes, dreams, and aspirations came crashing and crumbling around me.

To add to my despair, we had a gentleman in our church who sent word to me by one of the staff pastors, to "tell Pastor Pruett to get the sin out of his life and God will heal him." I did not need to take a guilt trip like that...yet, I did! I took the trip and wondered, "GOD WHAT KIND OF SIN COULD I HAVE COMMITTED THAT WOULD CAUSE SUCH A TRAGEDY TO HAPPEN TO ME? WAS IT MY SIN, OR WAS IT THE SIN OF MY PARENTS?"

I began to wake up at 2:00 and 3:00 in the morning, stumbling out of the bedroom into the living room, falling into a chair or couch, weeping my heart out, asking God to please reveal the sin that I might have committed to cause such a tragedy in my life.

Never will I forget, though I could not see my hand in front of my face, on one of those early hour experiences, the room brightly lit up with the Shekinah glory of God. You will know when you are in God's presence! I sensed arms go about my body. Whether they were the arms of an angel, or the Lord Himself, I really don't know, but at that moment I heard Him whisper to me, *"There is nothing between your soul and the Savior, and soon I would know something of His dealings with me in my life."*

So, I kept putting one foot in front of the other, and kept walking with God, knowing that He would reveal Himself to me in the course of time. On one of those mornings, I tuned to channel 30 in Los Angeles to listen to the DOMATA SERIES (which means "God's gifts to men").

I listened to a young man who

captured my attention as he began to talk about the KAIROS TIMES OF LIFE, or the various "seasons of life" that come to a child of God. He quoted the words of Jesus from the book of Luke, chapter 22, verse 31. *"Simon, Simon, behold Satan hath desired to have you that he may sift you as wheat, but I have prayed for you that your faith fail not and when thou art converted, strengthen the brethren."*

As I listened the speaker said, "It is more meaningful than the King James Version that we have at our disposal today. What Jesus literally said to Peter was: *"Simon, Simon, Satan hath demanded you for trial that he might make a sieve out of you; that he might show up the chaff of your life; that he can prove to those around you that you are not a follower of Mine. He wants to show up the inconsistencies of your life, Peter, but I have prayed for you...literally, I AM praying for you."*

May I suggest to you, Christian, the prayer for Peter was more than a good-night prayer like, "lay me down to sleep." The original language was, "I am agonizing for you, Peter. I am interceding for you, that your faith fail not in this KAIROS (uncertain) or particular season of your life. And when you are converted or changed, after much twisting and turning, then you will be able to minister to those who have problems in their lives."

You know, there is something about

the authority structure of God that satan, who is the adversary of mankind, still has the privilege to stand before God and accuse the brethren. He is known as the "accuser," and demands God's children for "trial." I have read in the Bible that satan is as a *"roaring lion, going about seeking whom he may devour."* You see, it is not until the book of Revelations that he is dehorned and dethroned; put into the pit, and ultimately into the Lake of Fire, and until then, we <u>do</u> have an adversary who as a roaring lion goes about seeking whom he may devour.

BUT HEAR ME! There is another Lion loose in the world, and He is the Lion of the tribe of Judah! He is sitting at the right hand of the Father. His present ministry is that of being an <u>advocate</u>, praying for your cause and mine into the ears of the Heavenly Father, and He prays with the same intensity as when He prayed for Peter. His plan for us is that we are to be VICTORIOUS IN EVERY CIRCUMSTANCE IN WHICH WE FIND OURSELVES.

Yes, **DEMANDED FOR TRIAL!** Let me suggest that the apostle Peter was not the only person in God's book who was demanded for trial. Job was "demanded for trial." He lost his wealth, his health, and all his children. But, because he remained true to God through his trying time...he did not regard iniquity in his heart nor did he charge God falsely...just read the last chapter of Job and see where God blessed him with greater wealth, greater health, and the same number of children filled his home. *"Though God slay me, yet will I trust Him...when He has tried me, I will come forth as pure Gold, tried in the fire."* HEAR ME, that sounds like a man who has victory in his life! He proved true in the dark circumstance of life.

Also, there were three Hebrew lads, Shadrach, Meschach, and Abednego. Their being "demanded for trial" took on another form..."the fiery furnace." It was heated seven times its normal heat, they were bound with new cords and thrown into the furnace because they would not bow their knees to some dumb image the king Nebuchadnezzar had erected.

The first thing that happened was a liberating experience, because all the cords were burned off! But, greater than this, was the privilege of walking with the fourth man, "who was like the Son of God." I wonder if we fail to realize in our fiery furnace experience that we are walking with the fourth man and He has promised to never leave us, even in the midst of the storm. His promise is, *"Fear not, for I have redeemed thee. I have called thee by name; thou art Mine. When thou passed through the fire thou were not burned. You will be like the Hebrew children, you will not even have the smell of smoke on you."* If you will follow the life of each of the Apostles, they were, on some occasion in their lives,

DEMANDED FOR TRIAL.

Let me share with you my personal testimony! As I stated, it was in 1976 I lost the sight in my right eye. Just three years later, I lost the sight in my left eye and was then declared legally blind. It was a traumatic time, and yet not all of life was down hill. I attended The Braille Institute in Los Angeles, learning Braille and studying psychology and typing.

These things kept me busy. I had a whole new way of life to learn. It was the month of September again. (I think I am going to skip the month of September from now on, for they are a little treacherous!) My brother Bob, pastor of our church, was preaching on Paul's thorn in the flesh...how

Paul had to make peace with that circumstance in his life before God could use him, and before he could resume his walk in the Lord. I was not buying it for a minute. I was tossing it over to the person behind me!

A "root" of bitterness had crept into my heart and I was beginning to resist what God was trying to do in my life. We left the church that day and Berna and I went to a nearby Cafe to eat our noon meal. We went through the line, sat down, mumbled a word of thanks, but I could not eat. I began to empty the bitterness and resistance and the unfairness of it all.

I thought of the life of Job and his problems that lasted only about nine months before he was on his way out of the valley, and I said, "GOD THIS HAS BEEN A YEAR AND ENOUGH IS TOO MUCH!" I could hear my wife softly weeping across the table. I thought, "How unfair," for it was she who put her arms around me and said, "We are going to make it through." It was she who read the scriptures to me over and over again, and taught me to eat off a plate I could not see; to dress myself, and to get back and forth to the church. So I apologized to her and we ate in silence.

At the close of the meal, I said I was going to walk home. (I had walked before, first with someone, and then alone.) She took the car and went home. I knew I had to hear from God! So, I took my white cane and began to tap my way along the Pacific Coast Highway in Lomita, California. I might have walked a block and a half when I heard a voice speaking to me.

I am not one to hear voices ordinarily. The voice said to me, "WHAT DO YOU HAVE IN YOUR HAND?"

I instinctively turned to my left because it was the direction the voice was coming from. Then, I stopped and waited. I thought surely someone would come and talk with me. When no one came, I turned and resumed tapping my way down the street.

I heard the voice again, "WHAT DO YOU HAVE IN YOUR HAND?" Immediately the Holy Spirit took me to another person in the Bible who was asked the very same question...Moses, after he had spent 40 years on the back side of the desert.

God began to speak to the heart of Moses saying, "I am not through with you yet. I have a job I want you to do." Moses began to make excuses as to how incapable he was such as an impediment of speech, but God already knew all that!

When God asked, "What do you have in your hand?" Moses said, "It is a rod."

God said, "Throw it down," and it became a serpent! The Bible says Moses was afraid of snakes and took off running!

"Pick it up by the tail, Moses," said God. He did and it became a rod again. God was simply saying to Moses, "It is ME, and I am not through with you. I have something more for you to do...this is not the back side of the desert anymore. I am ready for you to do My work in Israel." Moses submitted to the voice of the Lord.

As quickly as that story flashed through my mind, the Holy Spirit took me back again to a young stripling of a man on the back side of his father's farm, taking care of the ewe lambs. David was sent down also to take food to his brothers to see how the battle was faring against the Philistines. There he faced an impossible confrontation with a giant, who was shouting threats to Israel. Goliath was his name. Offended he would disrespect the God of Israel, he took five stones and stood on the battlefield willing to give God all he had.

David did not possess the armor of Saul or his weapons of warfare, but *he had the testimony of something he had proven in the past and he gave it to God*. What he had was just a little slingshot and some stones. He went out and God gave the battle to David and to Israel!

One more story flashed through my mind and that one was from Matthew's Gospel about a little boy with five loaves and two fishes and the question was asked, "WHAT ARE THEY AMONG SO MANY?" Yet, the boy was willing to give what he had to Jesus. Jesus was willing to receive them! He took the loaves and the fishes, blessed them, and fed the multitude numbering five thousand men, besides the women and children. After they ate, twelve basketfuls of the fragments were gathered!

I shall never forget the sound of that voice saying, "What do you have in your hand?" I knew I had to get home or they might put me into Harbor General Hospital in a strait jacket for weeping as I was before God. I realized God was dealing with me for He had something for me to do. It was there I had a prayer meeting and made a new commitment to God.

I thought I would never be able to preach the Gospel again. After all, I could not go to the pulpit without six to ten pages of notes and here I was blind. I made a commitment to God, "I will follow you."

The Lord said, "GIVE ME THE BROKENNESS OF YOUR LIFE."

I said, "Lord, you can have all of my life; my eyes, my whole frame for the rest of my days, and I will take every opportunity I have to share the claims of Christ to a world without God."

God answered, "GIVE ME THE BROKENNESS OF YOUR LIFE, AND I WILL USE IT TO TOUCH HUNDREDS AND THOUSANDS OF OTHERS WHO ARE BROKEN IN SOME AREA OF THEIR LIFE, AND I WILL RESTORE THEM!" That commitment has lasted six years now. I thank God for his goodness and grace in my life.

I know that some of you are hurting in some area of your life, or the Lord would not have awakened me this morning at 2:30 to pray for you and hold you up in prayer. I have asked God to touch you where you may be **"DEMANDED FOR TRIAL."** It may be in the area of relationships or in the area of finances. It may be in the area of physical that God would touch you and make you whole.

You may ask, "Do you believe in healing?"

I absolutely do, more than I ever have in my life...I <u>believe</u> in it. That is one of the areas the adversary wanted to defeat me; no one would want me to pray for them. I made a commitment that very day to pray for people, and God has been so gracious to heal, touch, and make whole.

If in some area of your life you are **"DEMANDED FOR TRIAL,"** know this...GOD LOVES YOU AND WITH A MILLION FLUID ARMS HE REACHES AROUND YOU! I want these arms to go about your life, to feel Him drawing you to Himself and to hear him whisper, "I love you. Even in the midst of the storm, I have victory for you and will bring you out!"

`Pastor Pruett died in 1985 eight days after preaching this sermon, but his testimony and legacy live on. I go to church with his wife, Berna, and she is an inspiration within herself. She is faithful, *helpful, and is always smiling. The world cannot give those attributes. I reread this testimony when I want a blessing. After 30 years it still is true.*

~Don Horne

Inspirational Songs, Poems

No Sorrows In Heaven

By Mrs. Cozadene Dawson-Martin-1958

Where I never more shall die. I am going over yonder

To that home beyond the sky.

Where I'll see my blessed Savior

Chorus:

In that home with all the angels

We will sing eternally

We'll be free from all temptations

When we sit at Jesus' feet.

No more sorrow over yonder

In that home we'll know no pain.

What a blessed happy meeting

When we crown Him King of Kings.

No more parting from our loved ones

No more sad good-byes to say.

For we'll be with one another

In that land of endless day.

Oh, What Joy!

By Mrs. Cozadene Dawson-Martin- 1959

With life's darkness all around me,

And no sunlight I can see

I just lift my eyes to Jesus

And He answers me.

Oh! What joy to know my Jesus!

Oh! What joy to know my Lord!

When I'm burdened down with sorrow

And I have no bright tomorrow

Then it's joy to know my Lord

Just to trust His Holy Word

Oh! 'Tis joy just to serve the Lord.

Each day will bring a blessing

If I'm holding to His hand.

No more sorrows will oppress me

Because He understands.

When life's long day is ended

And I lay my burdens down

I'll slip away to Jesus

To receive a golden crown.

He Understands

By Mrs. Cozadene Dawson-Martin- 1959

Chorus:

He understands, He knows each lonely heartache

He understands, He sees each tear that falls.

He understands, I know He'll guide me safely,

He understands, that's why I love Him so.

Tho' days are long and nights are dark and dreary,

His hand is there to guide me safely on.

I will trust in Him, tho' I am weak and
weary

I will lean on Him for I am not alone.

Each step I take my Saviour will go with
me

O'er mountain heights or in the valley
deep.

He's always there to comfort and direct
me

He understands, my life with Him will
be complete.

If He should call, would you obey His
pleading voice?

To walk with Him every mile of the way

He understands, He will go with you

He understands, give Him your heart today.

Walking With The King

By Mrs. Cozadene Dawson-Martin-
1962

Every hour of every day…

    My heart is filled with praise.

Just to know that I from sin have

    been set free.

Oh! The mercy of His Grace…

    And the power of His name!

He is now my everything…

    I'm walking with the King!

Chorus:

Walking with the King…

    He is my everything.

He saved my soul from sin…

    And made me pure within.

My heart doth now rejoice…

    Since I made my choice.

He is my everything…

    I'm walking with the King!

When troubles o'er me roll…

    On Jesus I can call.

To come and take these burdens…

    And fill my heart with song.

He's the beautiful Rose of Sharon…

    And Oh! I love Him so.

He is my everything…

    I'm walking with the King.

The Shepherd of Love

By Mrs. Cozadene Dawson-Martin

Taken from Reverend Carl Acorn's sermon
Sunday morning May 7, 1944

Oh! The peace and rest, that comes to
our heart

That only God can give.

No wonder we shout, no wonder we're
glad

For we'll live with Him for ever more.

Chorus:

Our Good Shepherd will lead us on and
on

And bathe our wounds in oil.

He'll carry us in His arms of love

To keep us from all pain and harm.

He's the one we love, who restores our soul

And mysterious may seem His way

He guides when we would all go wrong

But still He leads us on and on.

Tho' He leads us thru afflictions rare

Deep waters won't overflow us

When our burdens seem hard, so hard to bear,

He'll always be there, to lead us on.

Saviour Lead Me

Saviour, help me lest I stray
Guide my feet from day to day.
Let no harm over take my way
Saviour, lead me all the way.

There's a time when I feel low
Darkness seems to hover o'er
Sunshine soon will fade away
But it's Thee I need always.

There's another time I know
When brightness fills my heart aglow
Then I can feel my Saviour near
And know He's always there to cheer.
So as I travel day by day

Lord, keep me in the narrow way.

Help me win some soul to thee

That they your blessed face may see.

Saviour, lead me all the way

Guide my footsteps day by day

When my steps are getting slow

Lead me safely as I go.

This Wonderful Saviour of Mine

By Mrs. Cozadene Dawson-Martin- 1947

He's a rock of refuge to my troubled soul;

When I am in sorrow on Him my burdens I'll roll

He'll never leave me lonely, down hearted, or blue.

So I'll follow Him gladly, all the journey through.

Chorus:

I'll follow the Master wherever He leads.

Tho it be in the valley, or on the mountain steep

I'll sing His praise forever and tell of His love

For I'm on my way to heaven, that home above.

He's a wonderful Saviour, this friend of mine;

So constant and true, is His love divine.

He'll take away all my sorrow, and give me peace sublime.

This wonderful Saviour what a friend is mine.

What a friend is Jesus when the way seems dark;

He'll guide my every footstep, through this pilgrim way.

Wherever I wander, wherever I stray
My Saviour will go with me, all along the
way.

Have You Heard About My Jesus?

By Mrs. Cozadene Dawson-Martin-1958

Have you heard about my Jesus

And the awful thing they did?

They hung Him on a rugged cross

This Blessed Son of Man!

I'll serve this Blessed Son Of God

Throughout eternity!

*He went away to Heaven

To prepare a place for me.

He said, "I'll come again some day,"

His Blessed face I'll see.

He's coming at the midnight hour
So be sure to watch and pray
Or you will be forever doomed
On that eternal day.

When He comes again in Glory,
What a happy time t'will be!
To be resurrected with…
This Man of Galilee.
Oh! Such singing and such shouting
As you've never heard before,
Will all then take place
Upon the Golden Shore.

*Repeat

What Stones Do You Have?

www.ingramcontent.com/pod-product-compliance
Lightning Source LLC
Chambersburg PA
CBHW070951040426
42443CB00007B/457